FUNDAMENTAL
CONCEPTS IN
COMPUTER SCIENCE

Advances in Computer Science and Engineering: Texts

Editor-in-Chief: Erol Gelenbe *(Imperial College)*
Advisory Editors: Manfred Broy *(Technische Universitaet Muenchen)*
Gérard Huet *(INRIA)*

FUNDAMENTAL CONCEPTS IN COMPUTER SCIENCE

editors

Erol Gelenbe

*Member of the Turkish Academy of Sciences
and of Académie des Technologies
(French National Academy of Engineering)*

Jean-Pierre Kahane

*Member of the Académie des Sciences
(French National Academy of Sciences)*

Imperial College Press

ICP

Published by

Imperial College Press
57 Shelton Street
Covent Garden
London WC2H 9HE

Distributed by

World Scientific Publishing Co. Pte. Ltd.
5 Toh Tuck Link, Singapore 596224
USA office: 27 Warren Street, Suite 401-402, Hackensack, NJ 07601
UK office: 57 Shelton Street, Covent Garden, London WC2H 9HE

British Library Cataloguing-in-Publication Data
A catalogue record for this book is available from the British Library.

FUNDAMENTAL CONCEPTS IN COMPUTER SCIENCE
Advances in Computer Science and Engineerin: Texts — Vol. 3

ISBN-13 978-1-84816-290-7
ISBN-10 1-84816-290-1

Printed in Singapore.

PREFACE

Computer Science, or Informatics as it is often called in Europe, is viewed by many as being both a science and a technology. Clearly, its technological aspects are very much upon us on a day to day basis. Yet all other exact sciences such as physics, biology or chemistry are also very present in our daily lives through the technologies they generate, and yet we do not doubt that they have scientific foundations.

In some ways, Informatics is akin to a mathematical science, since formalisation, definition and deduction play an important role in the development of its concepts and in the embodiment of the concepts into artifacts. Informatics is also very similar to physics and engineering science, where models have to be linked to observation and measurement. Current research on computer networks and computer systems is an illustration of this second approach.

Some of the confusion about Informatics as a Science and as a Technology may arise from the fact that most of its pioneering contributors, many of whom are fortunately still alive, have actively contributed (and still do) to both the scientific principles, often based on mathematics, and to its technological and practical developments.

The links between computer arithmetic, which is based on algebra and algorithms, and digital circuit design are one example. The connection between mathematical models of queueing networks, which were originally inspired by telecommunications, computer systems and computer networks, and the commercial software tools that are used to analyse the performance of computer systems, and which incorporate these mathematical models, are another example. Yet another instance of this connection lies in the use of formal methods for the verification and testing of programs and software systems, which have enjoyed a long standing interaction with mathematical logic.

Much of the history of Informatics still remains to be written, and this effort can be undertaken after scholarly historians of science will have a better understanding of the field. However, aside from the original papers where seminal ideas were first presented, and surveys or discussions that appear at conferences and in a few specialised journals, the origins of the concepts in Informatics are not always well documented.

Furthermore, although basic concepts in Informatics are disseminated through educational programmes, the increasingly practical orientation of many undergraduate courses, and the increasing specialisation of many post-graduate courses, imply that pointers to the broad initial scientific concepts of Informatics are often not adequately transmitted to future generations. On the other hand, developments in computer technology, which are naturally far more "visible" both to the public and to students of the subject, are well documented both in every day life, in industry and commerce, in exhibits, and in specialised museums.

As we have already stated, we do believe that the writing of a history of Computer Science is best left to professional historians of science. However this book responds to an urgent need to grasp a unique opportunity, and to capitalise on the fact that contrary to the other sciences, many of the founders of Informatics are still professionally active.

This collection of essays is an attempt to reach out to Computer Scientists who wish to write about their own or others' seminal contributions, and we have been able to collect contributions representing a *broad* range of areas within Informatics. This volume has attracted a nice balance of papers, some with a theoretical outlook and others that concern significant practical developments. Most of the chapters are authored by the originators of the ideas and technologies themselves, while some are authored by computer scientists who have had a first-hand knowledge of the developments and of the pioneers whom they discuss.

The first chapter, devoted to a fundamental contribution by Corrado Bohm, one of the European pioneers of Computer Science, on Bohm's Theorem, relates to a fundamental and early result on program schemata, i.e. formalised flowcharts, and it is written by some of Bohm's distinguished students, Stefano Guerrini, Adolfo Piperno, and Mariangiola Dezani-Ciancaglini, with guidance from Prof. Bohm himself. The next chapter, on Membrane Computing is contributed by Prof. Gheorghe Păun, the person who actually launched the concepts in that area. The following chapter is authored by Giuseppe Longo, who discusses the distinction between simulation of nature based on highly causal computation, and nature itself in which non-determinism and randomness can play a dominant role. The fourth chapter is authored by the originator of a class of mathematical models called G-networks, together with colleagues who have made significant contributions to the subject; these are models of service systems (such as computer networks) as well as of neuronal networks, and it is shown these probabilistic models are also deterministic models of approximate computation. The next contribution by Tony Hoare, a pioneer of several areas of Informatics, including algorithms, programming methodology and parallel processing, discusses one of his important contributions to programming methods and to the verification of computer programmes. The fifth chapter is written by Steve Furber, a leading researcher and entrepreneur in computer processor technology, where he describes a processor technology based on a very successful design that has resulted in widespread use in commercial computing devices. The chapter on Carl Adam Petri is biographical nature, and also discusses the contributions and perspectives brought by Petri Nets. It is written by his eminent colleagues and friends Wilfried Brauer and Wolfgang Reisig, who have first hand knowledge of the contributions of this major pioneer. Jeff Buzen's chapter concerning some of the origins and successes of stochastic models of computer performance modelling is written by the person whose work gave rise to most of the basic algorithms used in this area. Jeff was also involved in bringing these techniques "to market" via a successful industrial venture. Finally, the last chapter by Olivier Pironneau on high performance computing, discusses the transformation that this field has effected on the design of aircraft and other modern transportation systems.

Most of the authors of this volume are members of their relevant National Academies, or of Academia Europaea, or both. Their articles in this volume express not only the fact that they have made imortant contributions to the field of Informatics, but that they also feel strongly about presenting the ideas and techniques that Informatics has generated and which need to be understood and appreciated by the scientific community and by future historians of the field.

We hope that this first volume will be followed by others that continue the presentation of Fundamental Concepts in Computer Science, through the eyes of the pioneers of this exciting field.

Erol Gelenbe
Member,
Turkish Academy
of Sciences, and French National
"Académie des Technologies"

Jean-Pierre Kahane
Member,
French Academy of Sciences

CONTENTS

Chapter 1

BÖHM'S THEOREM

STEFANO GUERRINI* and ADOLFO PIPERNO[†]

Dipartimento di Informatica
Università di Roma "La Sapienza"
Via Salaria 113, 00198 Roma, Italy
**guerrini@di.uniroma1.it*
†piperno@di.uniroma1.it

MARIANGIOLA DEZANI-CIANCAGLINI
Dipartimento di Informatica
Università di Torino, Corso Svizzera 185
10149 Torino, Italy
dezani@di.unito.it

1. Introduction

The technical significance of Böhm's theorem [3] suffices to deserve it a prominent place in any monograph on the theory of the λ-calculus [1, 22, 23] and makes it a basic result that any researcher working on λ-calculus must know. In addition to its technical content, we think that behind this beautiful result there is something of interest for a much wider audience. The clear thread that starting from his thesis [2] led Corrado Böhm to the research on λ-calculus and to the quest for an "internal" way to discriminate λ-terms, the deep analysis of the structures of λ-terms required by the proof of the theorem, the so-called Böhm-out technique, and the many unexpected consequences and applications of this technique [29] clearly put Böhm's theorem on a relevant position in the bookshelf of the main achievements of theoretical computer science. Moreover, as in the case of almost all the relevant results of Mathematics, the interest of Böhm's

---

Under the exceptional guidance of Corrado Böhm.

theorem is not only in the statement that it asserts, but also, and maybe mainly, in the constructions required by its proof.

As we already mentioned, Böhm's theorem is one of the main results of the theory of λ-calculus. Looking at the theorem from a computer science perspective, it states that the extensional equivalence of λ-calculus "normal forms" may be defined by means of a syntactic equivalence. More precisely, let us interpret λ-terms as programs, assuming that two programs/λ-terms are equivalent when they behave in the same way on all the inputs (extensional equivalence); then, it is a consequence of Böhm's theorem that two programs/λ-terms in "normal form" are equivalent if and only if they are written in the same way (syntactic equivalence), apart for some expansions corresponding to the so-called η-equivalence of λ-terms (which is easily decidable). Let us remark that when we say "on all the inputs", we mean "on all the λ-terms", since we are in an untyped setting and any λ-term can be the argument of any other λ-term.

By the way, Böhm's theorem does not imply at all that in the λ-calculus the equivalence of programs is decidable: the equivalence of two λ-terms (not in normal form) was the first problem for which undecidability could be proved [13], even before the undecidability of the halting problem [43]. In fact, in the 1930s, Church proposed the λ-calculus as a foundational system for mathematical logic [12]. Then, while his former student Kleene analyzed the notion of λ-definability, showing that every recursive function can be coded (by means of "normal forms") into the λ-calculus [26, 27], Church related the notion of effective calculability to that of recursive function, and then of λ-definability, proving at the same time that the equivalence of two λ-terms (not in normal form) is undecidable [13]. Immediately after the work of Church, Turing introduced his machine approach to computation and proved the undecidability of the halting problem [43]; then, he also proved the equivalence between his notion of computability and that of λ-definable function [44].

In λ-calculus, programs/λ-terms are constructed in a purely functional way, and there is no distinction between programs and data: every program can be passed as the argument of another program. The evaluation mechanism, the so called β-rule, mimics the operation of replacing equally labeled formal placeholders with a specific λ-term, neither looking at its actual structure nor if the places are for functions or for arguments. A λ-term is in normal form when it cannot be reduced any further, by the application of the β-rule, implicitly declaring the end of the evaluation process. Being the ending results of the evaluation of a λ-term (when this evaluation terminates), normal forms play the role of *values* and Böhm's theorem ensures that two values are equal only if they are written in the same way.

In λ-calculus, the normal form, if any, of a term is unique; in other words, the result of a computation is independent of the order in which the computational steps are applied. Because of this, normal forms can be seen as the "denotations" of λ-terms, or equivalently, as their primary meaning. Böhm's theorem ensures that in λ-calculus, every denotation of a λ-term (if we limit to programs/λ-terms that terminate) can be written in only one way: two syntactically distinct values/normal forms correspond in fact to two distinct denotations. Such a property makes the λ-calculus an ideal mathematical model in which to interpret programs and in which to study their properties — in particular, their equivalence. Moreover, Böhm's theorem ensures that the way in which we can separate two distinct λ-terms is internal to the calculus; it suffices to apply the distinct λ-terms to the same suitable sequence of inputs. The construction of such a sequence of inputs requires the determination of a set of combinatory operations on the tree structure of λ-terms that are at the basis of the so-called Böhm-out technique (see Section 2). Proving his theorem, Corrado Böhm not only recognized the basic operations of the Böhm-out technique, but also had the great intuition that such combinatory operations could be internalized into the λ-calculus by means of suitable λ-terms. Such a deep understanding of the computational mechanism behind the β-rule was a great breakthrough in the analysis of the basic computational mechanisms of programs and played a central role in the development of the mathematical studies of the semantics of programs (see Section 4 on the follow-up to Böhm's theorem).

The idea that an interesting computational system should have enough power to be able to speak about itself has played a central role in all the research works of Corrado Böhm, not only in his studies on λ-calculus, but also in his thesis [2]. Corrado Böhm defined the first compiler that could be described in its own language (see also Ref. 28) in his thesis. Since then, one of the main questions that guided Corrado Böhm in his research on computational systems was, "how much of its meta-theory is contained into the system itself?" Therefore, when he started to think at the λ-calculus as a basis for defining programming languages (actually, he believes that the λ-calculus is THE programming language), one of the first questions that he tried to answer was if there was an internal way for studying the equality of λ-terms, and the answer was Böhm's theorem.

This note is organized as follows: in Section 2, we explain Böhm's theorem in an informal way using trees, while in Section 3, we introduce the λ-calculus in order to properly formulate Böhm's theorem. Finally, Section 4 gives an overview of the impressive research activity which originated from Böhm's theorem.

2. Böhm's Theorem for Trees

Assume that we are given two disjoint sets of labels, namely a set $\mathcal{L} = \{A, B, C, \dots\}$, and a set $\ell = \{a, b, c, \dots\}$. We consider the set $\mathcal{T}$ of *trees* labeled with elements from $\mathcal{L} \cup \ell$, with the restriction that, for any $T \in \mathcal{T}$ and for any $x \in \ell$, the label x appears at most once in T.

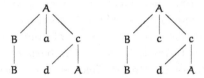

In the example given above, the first tree is an element of $\mathcal{T}$, while the second one is not in $\mathcal{T}$, since the label c appears twice in it.

A notion of equivalence is established over elements of $\mathcal{T}$: two trees $T_1, T_2 \in \mathcal{T}$ are *equivalent* if they are equal or they both can be made equal to a tree $T \in \mathcal{T}$ by adding nodes, labeled in ℓ, as rightmost sons of some nodes. In such a case, we say that T_1 and T_2 *expand* to T. Clearly, both T_1 and T_2 are equivalent to T.

As an example, the first two trees in the following figure are equivalent, since they both expand to the third one.

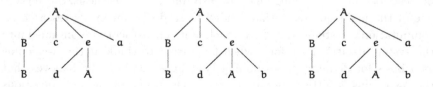

The defined equivalence is relevant since it allows, when comparing trees, to abstract from their structure. In effect, given $T_1, T_2 \in \mathcal{T}$, there always exist $T_1', T_2' \in \mathcal{T}$, having the same tree structure, such that T_i is equivalent to T_i' $(i = 1, 2)$.

A *tree transformation* is an operator which, when substituted to a label, rearranges its sons according to some rule. We will use tree transformations of three different kinds:

Replacement: REPLACE(k, S), where $S \in \mathcal{T}$, is the operator which takes k subtrees, discards them and returns the tree S:

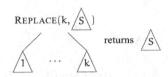

Selection: SELECT(k, i) is the operator which takes k subtrees and returns the ith one:

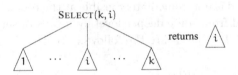

Rotation: ROTATE(k) is the operator which takes $k + 1$ subtrees, where the $k + 1$th one is a leaf and its label is from ℓ, and moves the $k + 1$th up to the root:

Böhm's theorem (rephrased): Let $S_1, S_2 \in \mathcal{T}$ be arbitrary trees. Then for every pair of non-equivalent trees, $T_1, T_2 \in \mathcal{T}$, there exist $T_1', T_2' \in \mathcal{T}$ such that:

(1) T_1' is equivalent to T_1 and T_2' is equivalent to T_2;

(2) there exist tree operations which *discriminate* T_1' from T_2', transforming any tree with the same structure of T_1' and equivalent to T_1 into S_1, and

any tree with the same structure of T_2' and equivalent to T_2 into S_2, respectively.

We proceed modulo the previously defined equivalence relation over trees, thus assuming that the trees to be discriminated have the same structure. The proof of the theorem is split into three cases:

A simple case: Let $T_1, T_2 \in \mathcal{T}$ be such that their roots have different labels, say A and B, respectively, as in the following example:

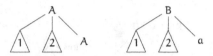

then the substitution $A \leftarrow \text{REPLACE}(3, S_1), B \leftarrow \text{REPLACE}(3, S_2)$ transforms T_1 into S_1 and T_2 into S_2.

Information extraction: In general, the difference between the two trees to be discriminated is not immediately visible at the roots. Such information must be extracted from some deeper level by means of selection operators. As an example, if $T_1, T_2 \in \mathcal{T}$ are the following trees:

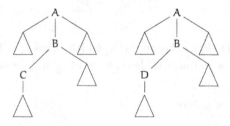

then the substitution:

$$A \leftarrow \text{SELECT}(3, 2), B \leftarrow \text{SELECT}(2, 1),$$
$$C \leftarrow \text{REPLACE}(1, S_1), D \leftarrow \text{REPLACE}(1, S_2)$$

transforms T_1 into S_1 and T_2 into S_2.

The hard case: In the previous example, the labels C and D have been easily extracted from the trees using suitable selectors. This is not immediately feasible in the following example:

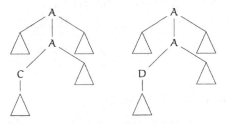

since the same selector, when substituted to different occurrences of A, is now required to have two different behaviors; namely, in the topmost occurrence, it must select the second of three subtrees, in the second occurrence it must select the first of two subtrees. To solve this case, we first consider the trees $T_1', T_2' \in \mathcal{T}$, equivalent to T_1 and T_2, respectively:

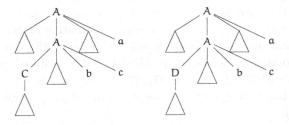

We then apply the substitution $A \leftarrow \text{ROTATE}(3)$, thus obtaining the following trees, which can be discriminated as in the previous case.

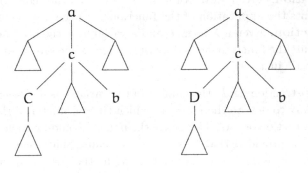

In fact the substitution

$$a \leftarrow \text{SELECT}(3,2), c \leftarrow \text{SELECT}(3,1),$$
$$C \leftarrow \text{REPLACE}(1, S_1), D \leftarrow \text{REPLACE}(1, S_2),$$

transforms T_1 into S_1 and T_2 into S_2.

3. Böhm's Theorem for λ-Calculus

The λ-calculus, also sometimes referred to as the calculus of λ-notation, was introduced by Alonzo Church in the 1930s [12]. In the attempt to give a complete system for the foundations of mathematics, Church took as primitive the notion of function instead of that of set. Even if the foundational project failed, because of the fact that the Russell's paradox of "the set of all sets that do not contain themselves as members" can be reformulated in the λ-calculus, Church used the λ-calculus to start the study of computability. In particular, by proving that the equivalence of two λ-terms is undecidable [13], Church gave the first problem for which undecidability could be proved, even before the halting problem [43]. Since then, the λ-calculus has played a relevant role in the development of theoretical computer science, in particular, it has inspired programming languages like LISP [30, 39] and ML [21, 31, 32] and has proved to be a fundamental tool in the analysis of the semantics of programming languages [34, 41, 42, 46].

The main idea of the λ-calculus is that every expression of the calculus, i.e. every λ-term, stands for a function. λ-terms are built from variables, the basic elements of the calculus, in two ways:

(i) **application**: given two λ-terms T and S, the composition TS represents the application of the function T to the argument S;

(ii) **abstraction**: given a λ-term T and a variable x, the abstraction $\lambda x.T$ represents the function defined by the λ-term T viewed as an expression parametric in x.

In an abstraction $\lambda x.T$, the name x of the variable is no longer relevant, but just a way to denote the places in which the parameter of the function built by abstraction occurs. Therefore, the name x could be replaced by any other name y, provided that this would not cause that some occurrences of y in T be improperly associated with the renamed abstraction (e.g., in $\lambda x.xy$, the x can be renamed by z getting the equivalent λ-term $\lambda z.zy$, but it cannot be renamed by y, that would lead to $\lambda y.yy$). The equivalence induced by variable renaming is the so-called α-congruence.

A λ-term is *closed* if all its variables are abstracted.

The only "computational rule" of the λ-calculus is the β-rule that, given the application of an abstraction $\lambda x.T$ to S, replaces S to every occurrence of the variable x in T (this may also require some variable renaming in order to avoid that the variables in S not associated with any abstraction might be "captured" by some abstraction in T). A λ-term is in *normal form* when it cannot be transformed (reduced) by means of the β-rule.

The β-equivalence is the equivalence relation induced on λ-terms by the β-reduction, assuming that two λ-terms are equivalent when they are the same λ-term or when they can be β-reduced to equivalent λ-terms (equivalently, the β-equivalence is the congruence generated by the reflexive, symmetric and transitive closure of the β-rule).

The η-equivalence is the equivalence obtained by assuming that given a λ-term T, if we apply it to a fresh variable x and we construct then the abstraction $\lambda x.Tx$, we obtain a function that is equivalent to T. In fact, the two functions are extensionally equivalent, since the application of $\lambda x.Tx$ to any λ-term S, immediately reduces to TS by using the β-rule, namely $(\lambda x.Tx)S$ β-reduces to T.

Böhm's theorem says that the equational theory induced by the β-reduction is complete for its normal forms. In fact, trying to equate any pair of non-η-equivalent normal λ-terms would correspond to equating the whole set of the normal λ-terms, forcing the collapse of the whole set of λ-terms into one point.

Normal forms have a structure which is similar to that of the trees as defined in Section 2. The η-equivalence corresponds to the equivalence defined over those trees and a representation of normal forms can be obtained by adding abstractions in suitable positions: the λ-calculus expert can recognize the so-called *Böhm trees* (see Section 4.4). The tree operations in Section 2 can be represented by λ-terms, so that the discrimination algorithm for closed normal forms can be *internalized*: it can be performed by objects of the calculus itself. For instance, the operators REPLACE(k, S), SELECT(k, i) and ROTATE(k) correspond to the λ-terms

$$\lambda x_1 \cdots x_k \cdot S, \quad \lambda x_1 \cdots x_k \cdot x_i \quad \text{and} \quad \lambda x_1 \cdots x_{k+1} \cdot x_{k+1} x_1 \cdots x_k,$$

respectively. We are now able to state Böhm's theorem in its original form:

Theorem [3]: *Let Λ_N^0 be the set of closed normal forms, and let S_1 and S_2 be arbitrary λ-terms. For any non-η-equivalent terms $T_1, T_2 \in \Lambda_N^0$ there exists a λ-term Δ such that the application of Δ to T_1 evaluates to S_1 and the application of Δ to T_2 evaluates to S_2.*

4. Follow-Up to Böhm's Theorem

The semantics of a programming language gives meanings to programs. This can be done in two different ways: *operationally*, providing a way in which programs are evaluated; *denotationally*, defining an interpretation of programs into a *model*, a mathematical structure which is constructed in order to be able to describe some desired computational properties. A huge amount of research has derived from the result and from the technique of Böhm's theorem, characterizing relevant properties of λ-terms, from both the operational and the denotational perspectives.

4.1. *Böhm's work on Böhm's theorem*

Corrado Böhm himself, together with some of his collaborators, has continued investigating discriminability of λ-terms, essentially from an operational perspective. In Ref. 5 a finite set of closed normal forms pairwise non-η-equivalents are discriminated. In Ref. 7 the proof of the theorem is revisited according to some restrictions on the shape of the discriminating solution. The notion of X-*separability* has been introduced in Ref. 10 and then characterized in Ref. 8. In some sense, X-separability avoids the use of rotation operators at the outer level of λ-terms, introducing the set X of variables to be substituted by operators. The notion of X-separability has interesting relationships with invertibility of λ-terms. The Böhm-out technique is the basis of the implementation, presented in Ref. 9, of the CuCh-machine, a λ-calculus interpreter introduced by Böhm and Gross in Ref. 6.

4.2. *Generalizations of Böhm's theorem*

The first generalizations of Böhm's theorem considered the pure λ-calculus. Wadsworth [45] extended Böhm's theorem to two arbitrary λ-terms which are different in Scott's D_∞ model [38]. We already mentioned [5] in previous subsection. Finally in Ref. 14 the discriminability of a finite set of arbitrary λ-terms is characterized. The original Böhm's theorem and this last generalization are essentially the content of Section 10.4 in Ref. 1. The discrimination of infinite sets of λ-terms has been studied in Refs. 35, 36, 40.

Successively, the λ-calculus has been extended or immersed in other languages in order to obtain finer observations on the behavior of λ-terms. Sangiorgi [37] considers the encoding of λ-calculus in the π-calculus, a calculus of mobile processes, and the addition of a unary non-deterministic operator. A notion of resource is the extension considered in Ref. 11, while Refs. 16 and 20 add a binary parallel operator and a non-deterministic choice. All the above-mentioned extensions are equivalent from the point of view of discriminability. A weaker discriminability result is obtained by adding to the λ-calculus a binary non-deterministic choice and a numeral system in Ref. 18. A finer discriminability is presented in Ref. 19 by means of two suitable projection operators.

4.3. Theories and models of λ-calculus

One immediate consequence of Böhm's theorem is that the theory of η-equivalence for closed normal forms is Hilbert-Post complete, i.e. given two arbitrary λ-terms $T_1, T_2 \in \Lambda_N^0$, either they are η-equivalent or the theory obtained by adding the equality $T_1 = T_2$ is inconsistent (see Corollary 10.4.3 of Ref. 1).

Therefore, no consistent model of λ-calculus can equate non-η-equivalent closed normal forms.

Similarly, the generalization of Böhm's theorem of Ref. 45 (already mentioned in Section 4.2), implies that the theory of Scott's D_∞ model [38] turns out to be maximal [45].

4.4. Böhm trees and Böhm-out-technique

The paramount historical importance of Böhm's theorem lies in the fact, already stressed by the author in the original paper and afterwards pointed out by various researchers, that its proof is constructive; an elegant implementation in categorical abstract machine language (CAML) is given in Ref. 24.

Exactly, the original proof of Böhm's theorem has inspired a representation of normal forms as trees, similar to the representation discussed in Section 2, which was first introduced in Ref. 4 and then discussed in Ref. 15. Barendregt [1] extended this representation to arbitrary λ-terms and called Böhm trees the so-obtained trees. Barendregt also called Böhm-out-technique essentially the tree operators on trees that we introduced in Section 2. Other trees have been proposed to represent λ-terms: a recent survey can be found in Ref. 25, where Böhm trees for term rewriting systems are studied. The representation of closed normal forms of Ref. 4 has been later used in Ref. 35 in order to express Böhm's theorem as a non-equality predicate over the algebra of normal forms.

4.5. *Observational equivalence*

In the same year as Böhm's theorem [3], Morris [33] for the first time defined a notion of an observational or contextual equivalence, which was going to have such important developments in more recent years, particularly in the domain of interactive concurrent computing: two λ-terms were defined equivalent if, whenever they are put in the same context, either they both make it reducible to a normal form or they both make it divergent. Böhm's theorem can then be viewed as stating that such an observational equivalence coincides, for normal forms, with η-equivalence. A survey on the relations between Böhm's theorem and observational equivalence is found in Ref. 17.

References

[1] H. Barendregt, *The Lambda Calculus, Its Syntax and Semantics*. Revised edition (North-Holland Publishing Co., Amsterdam, NL, 1984).
[2] C. Böhm, Calculatrices digitales. Du d'Echiffrage des Formules Mathématiques par la Machine Même dans la Conception du Programme. *Annali di Matematica Pura e Applicata* 4(37) (1954) 1–51.
[3] C. Böhm, Alcune Proprietà delle Forme Normali nel K-calcolo. *Technical Report 696* (INAC, Roma, Italy, 1968).
[4] C. Böhm and M. Dezani-Ciancaglini, Combinatorial problems, combinator equations and normal forms, in *ICALP'74*, volume 14 of *Lecture Notes in Computer Science*, ed. J. Loeckx (Springer-Verlag, Berlin, Germany, 1974), pp. 185–199.
[5] C. Böhm, M. Dezani-Ciancaglini, P. Peretti and S. Ronchi della Rocca, A discrimination algorithm inside lambda-calculus. *Theor. Comput. Sci.* 8(3) (1978) 271–291.

[6] C. Böhm and W. Gross, Introduction to the CUCH, in *Automata Theory*, ed. R. Caianiello (Academic Press, London, UK, 1966), pp. 35–65.

[7] C. Böhm and A. Piperno, Surjectivity for finite sets of combinators by weak reduction, in *CSL'87*, volume 329 of *Lecture Notes in Computer Science*, eds. E. Börger, H. K. Büning and M. M. Richter (Springer-Verlag, Berlin, Germany, 1987), pp. 27–43.

[8] C. Böhm and A. Piperno, Characterizing X-separability and one-side invertibility in lambda-beta-omega-calculus, in *LICS'88*, ed. Y. Gurevich (IEEE Computer Society Press, New York, NY, USA, 1988), pp. 91–101.

[9] C. Böhm, A. Piperno and S. Guerrini, Lambda-definition of function(al)s by normal forms, in *ESOP'94*, volume 788 of *Lecture Notes in Computer Science*, ed. D. Sannella (Springer-Verlag, Berlin, Germany, 1994), pp. 135–149.

[10] C. Böhm and E. Tronci, X-separability and left-invertibility in lambda-calculus, in *LICS'87*, ed. D. Gries (IEEE Computer Society Press, New York, NY, USA, 1987), pp. 320–328.

[11] G. Boudol and C. Laneve, The discriminating power of multiplicities in the λ-calculus, *Inform. Comput.* **126**(1) (1996) 83–102.

[12] A. Church, A set of postulates for the foundation of logic, *Ann. Math.* **33** (1932) 346–366.

[13] A. Church, An unsolvable problem of elementary number theory, *Am. J. Math.* **58** (1936) 345–363.

[14] M. Coppo, M. Dezani-Ciancaglini and S. R. D. Rocca, (Semi)-separability of finite sets of terms in Scott's D_∞-models of the lambda-calculus, in *ICALP'78*, volume 62 of *Lecture Notes in Computer Science*, eds. G. Ausiello and C. Böhm (Springer-Verlag, Berlin, Germany, 1978), pp. 142–164.

[15] H. B. Curry, On a polynomial representation of λβ-normal forms, in *Konstruktionen versus Positionen*, ed. K. Lorenz (Walter de Gruyter, Berlin, Germany, 1979), pp. 94–98.

[16] M. Dezani-Ciancaglini, U. de'Liguoro and A. Piperno, Filter models for conjunctive-disjunctive λ-calculi, *Theor. Comput. Sci.* **170**(1–2) (1996) 83–128.

[17] M. Dezani-Ciancaglini and E. Giovannetti, From Böhm's theorem to observational equivalences: an informal account, in *BOTH'01*, volume 50 of *Electronic Notes in Theoretical Computer Science*, ed. J.-J. Lévy (Elsevier, New York, NY, USA, 2001), pp. 83–116.

[18] M. Dezani-Ciancaglini, B. Intrigila and M. Venturini-Zilli, Böhm's theorem for Böhm trees, in *ICTCS'98*, eds. P. Degano and U. Vaccaro (World Scientific, Oxford, UK, 1998), pp. 1–23.

[19] M. Dezani-Ciancaglini, P. Severi and F.-J. de Vries, Infinitary lambda calculus and discrimination of Berarducci trees, *Theor. Comput. Sci.* **298**(2) (2003) 275–302.

[20] M. Dezani-Ciancaglini, J. Tiuryn and P. Urzyczyn, Discrimination by parallel observers: the algorithm, *Inform. Comput.* **150**(2) (1999) 153–186.

[21]   M. J. C. Gordon, R. Milner, L. Morris, M. C. Newey and C. P. Wadsworth, A metalanguage for interactive proof in LCF, in *POPL'78*, ed. T. G. Szymanski (ACM Press, New York, NY, USA, 1978), pp. 119–130.

[22]   C. Hankin, *Lambda Calculi: A Guide for Computer Scientists* (Oxford University Press, Oxford, UK, 1995).

[23]   J. Hindley and J. P. Seldin, *Introduction to Combinators and λ-Calculus* (Cambridge University Press, Cambridge, UK, 1986).

[24]   G. Huet, An analysis of Böhm's theorem, *Theor. Comput. Sci.* **121**(1–2) (1993) 145–167.

[25]   J. Ketema, Böhm-like trees for rewriting, PhD thesis, Vrije Universiteit Amsterdam, Amsterdam, NL, 2006.

[26]   S. Kleene, A theory of positive integers in formal logic, *Am. J. Math.* **57** (1935) 153–173 and 219–244.

[27]   S. Kleene, Lambda-definability and recursiveness, *Duke Math. J.* **2** (1936) 340–353.

[28]   D. E. Knuth and L. T. Pardo, The early development of programming languages, in *A History of Computing in the Twentieth Century*, eds. N. Metropolis, J. Howlett and G.-C. Rota (Academic Press, London, UK, 1980).

[29]   J. J. Lévy, *BOTH'01: Böhm's Theorem: Applications to Computer Science Theory*, volume 50 of *Electronic Notes in Theoretical Computer Science* (Elsevier, New York, NY, USA, 2001).

[30]   J. McCarthy, Recursive functions of symbolic expressions and their computation by machine, Part I, *Commun. ACM* **3**(4) (1960) 184–195.

[31]   R. Milner, A proposal for standard ML, in *LISP and Functional Programming*, eds. E. S. Schneider, J. Guy and L. Steele (ACM Press, New York, NY, USA, 1984), pp. 184–197.

[32]   R. Milner, M. Tofte, R. Harper and D. Macqueen, *The Definition of Standard ML — Revised* (MIT Press, Cambridge, MA, USA, 1997).

[33]   J. H. Morris, Lambda calculus models of programming languages, PhD thesis, MIT, Cambridge, MA, USA, 1968.

[34]   B. C. Pierce, *Types and Programming Languages* (MIT Press, Cambridge, MA, USA, 2002).

[35]   A. Piperno, An algebraic view of the Böhm-out technique, *Theor. Comput. Sci.* **212**(1–2) (1999) 233–246.

[36]   S. Ronchi della Rocca, Discriminability of infinite sets of terms in the D_∞-models of the λ-calculus, in *CAAP'81*, volume 112 of *Lecture Notes in Computer Science*, eds. E. Astesiano and C. Böhm (Springer-Verlag, Berlin, Germany, 1981), pp. 40–54.

[37]   D. Sangiorgi, The lazy lambda calculus in a concurrency scenario, *Inform. Comput.* **111**(1) (1994) 120–153.

[38]   D. Scott, Continuous lattices, in *Toposes, Algebraic Geometry and Logic*, volume 274 of *Lecture Notes in Mathematics*, ed. F. Lawvere (Springer-Verlag, Berlin, Germany, 1972), pp. 97–136.

[39]   P. Seibel, *Practical Common Lisp* (Apress, Berkeley, CA, USA, 2005).

[40] R. Statman and H. Barendregt, Böhm's theorem, Church's delta, numeral systems, and Ershov morphisms, *Processes, Terms and Cycles: Steps on the Road to Infinity*, volume 3838 of *Lecture Notes in Computer Science*, eds. A. Middeldorp, V. van Oostrom, F. van Raamsdonk and R. de Vrijer (Springer-Verlag, Berlin, Germany, 2005), pp. 40–54.

[41] J. E. Stoy, *Denotational Semantics: The Scott-Strachey Approach to Programming Language Semantics* (MIT Press, Cambridge, MA, USA, 1997).

[42] R. D. Tennent, The denotational semantics of programming languages, *Commun. ACM* **19**(8) (1976) 437–453.

[43] A. Turing, On computable numbers, with an application to the Entscheidungsproblem, *Proceedings of the London Mathematical Society* **42**(2) (1936) 230–265; correction ibid. **43** (1937) 544–546.

[44] A. Turing, Computability and λ-definability, *J. Symb. Logic* **2** (1937) 153–163.

[45] C. P. Wadsworth, The relation between computational and denotational properties for Scott's D_∞-models of the lambda-calculus. *SIAM J. Comput.* **5**(3) (1976) 488–521.

[46] G. Winskel, *The Formal Semantics of Programming Languages, an Introduction* (MIT Press, Cambridge, MA, USA, 1993).

Chapter 2

MEMBRANE COMPUTING: HISTORY AND BRIEF INTRODUCTION

GHEORGHE PĂUN

Institute of Mathematics of the Romanian Academy
PO Box 1-764, 014700 Bucureşti, Romania
and

Department of Computer Science and Artificial Intelligence
University of Sevilla
Avda. Reina Mercedes s/n, 41012 Sevilla, Spain
george.paun@imar.ro, gpaun@us.es

At the moment when these notes are written, membrane computing is only eight years old. Is this an age when a "history" can be recalled? The doubt suggested by the mere formulation of this question is removed by the personal feeling that, actually, the domain has a *long* history, a feeling grounded on the large number of notions, research directions, results, applications, publications, and events related to membrane computing. The second part of these notes will (try to) prove these assertions, providing the reader with a quick introduction to membrane computing, pointing out mainly basic ideas and types of results and of applications. Before that, the first part of the paper, provides a personal view about these last (more than) eight years, remembering facts which might not have a great significance for somebody not involved in this field or not knowing the persons which will be mentioned below, but significant for me. This is, indeed, a *personal history* of membrane computing.

Consequently, the reader is asked not to evaluate this text with modest/non-modest measures. I used to say several times (e.g. in interviews for Romanian newspapers) that, while everybody tries to become a *name* in science, I "failed", because I just became a letter: the computing devices studied in membrane computing are called *P systems*. It is not easy to become a letter and then to discuss about it in conferences or in texts like the present one, but, at the same time, your vanity is highly pleased when doing it. This should be the same for everybody, the only difference being that customarily the people do not admit that they are vanitous. Moreover, in general, the scientists are not modest, and mathematicians still less. Pretending to be exact, they promote themselves, without any thought paid to any shame, because no thought is paid to any self-promotion. The same with my recollections here: I will just try to be exact.

1. Personal Views on the History of Membrane Computing

1.1. *The pre-history*

In some sense, everything goes back to the seventies of the last century. I was then a student of the contagious Professor Solomon Marcus, at the Faculty of Mathematics of the University of Bucharest. I was dreaming to become a teacher in a high school (not any one, but *the one* from Curtea de Argeş, a picturesque small town on the Argeş river, close to Carpathians), but I became a researcher in language theory after meeting Marcus. Explicitly or implicitly, Marcus induced me the conviction that "everything can be described by a (formal) language", with a great part of the research in our group done at that time under the slogan "linguistics as a pilot science". I was at the same time lucky to get a copy of Arto Salomaa's book *Formal Languages*, published in 1973 by the Academic Press. Years later, Marcus used to say something like "this was the book which gave the name to the domain". Influential, indeed. Crystal-clear, written perfectly from a didactic point of view, with a wise selection and arrangement of the material. I was definitely (de)formed by this book; it was probably the only mathematical book which I have almost completely read just for the pleasure of reading it, and later it was no way to escape from its influence. I became a formal language theorist in the Marcus-Salomaa sense.

Anticipating the story, I had the privilege to remain around Marcus until now, and, after (the changes from Romania in) 1989, I also had the privilege to work with Salomaa (and with his "brother" — Grzegorz Rozenberg), also until now (and, I hope, still for a long future).

Already in the seventies, Marcus wrote about the use of linguistics and formal languages in the study of genome, but at that time I was more interested in the applications of formal grammars in modeling economic processes — the topic of my PhD thesis and of my first book, published in 1980 in Romanian.

Looking backwards, almost everything which I have studied in the "old times" was useful to membrane computing, everything was a sort of preparation of tools for it. For instance, I have spent many years investigating grammars with restrictions in derivations, especially matrix grammars — the first universality proof (well, the second, see below) about P systems was based on matrix grammars with appearance checking in the strong binary normal form. I mention on purpose all these technical terms, in order to point out the level of technicality/detail at which this link between the two domains is established. The research on this topic was concluded with a monograph, written together with Jürgen Dassow (Magdeburg, Germany — initially, East Germany, hence possible for me to visit in the communist time) and published in 1989 by Springer-Verlag. Another "campaign" was devoted to grammar systems, sets of grammars cooperating according to a specified protocol in generating a unique language. Again, a monograph has concluded that work (Gordon and Breach, 1994, in collaboration with Erzsébet Csuhaj-Varjú from Hungary, J. Dassow from Germany, and Jozef Kelemen from the Czech Republic).

An important stage after that was devoted to DNA computing.

A parenthesis: I sometimes believe that someone's life and career are a series of lucky or non-lucky events, that we live in a "multiverse" (M. Gell–Mann term), which is actualized in one particular "universe" just by chance. I can illustrate this belief with many happenings from my life, including the involvement in DNA computing.

In April 1991 (Arto remembers also the day, I only remember the meeting with him in the Turku railway station, after two days and three nights spent in the train, from Bucharest to Chişinău, Moscow, Leningrad, Helsinki, Turku), I visited for the first time the group of Salomaa, in Turku. In 1992–1993, I was mainly in Magdeburg, Germany, as a fellow of the Alexander von Humboldt Foundation, then from 1994 I started a long stay in Turku. Practically, until 1999, I have spent more than half of each year in Finland. I was there together with the late Alexandru Mateescu, Sandu for friends (he passed away in January 2005). Sandu mentioned me once about problems of combinatorics on words related to the genome project, and he has also shown to me some papers of this kind. I did not like any of them, they were not dealing with languages and grammars, and I was not impressed at all. But in April 1994 (I think it was in April — I can check, but I will not do, Arto will correct me if I am wrong), I was visiting Vienna, at the invitation of a great friend, Rudi Freund, and from Vienna I have also gone to Graz, where a symposium was held in honor of Arto Salomaa, on the occasion of his 60th birthday. Somebody — I think that it was Lila Kari, a former student of mine, who had completed a brilliant PhD with Arto and after that moved to Canada, to London Ontario — brought to Sandu several new papers about DNA and languages, including a paper by Tom Head (published in 1987, hence not so new).

This paper made history, as marking the beginning of (theoretical) DNA computing. Seven years before the seminal experiment of L. M. Adleman, of solving a small instance of the Hamiltonian path problem in a laboratory, by handling DNA molecules in the same way — but with

other goals — as the biochemists used to do it, Tom Head introduced the
splicing operation, a language-theoretic model of the recombinant behavior
of DNA molecules under the influence of restriction enzymes and ligase
enzymes. I was immediately conquered by the novelty and elegance of this
operation — so much conquered that the next five years I have done almost
nothing else. Actually, the enthusiasm was complete only after proving that
splicing systems (together with Salomaa and Rozenberg, I have called them
H systems, in honor of Tom Head) can compute whatever a Turing machine
can compute. Well, this happens when the rules are controlled in various
ways, suggested by regulated rewriting and not too much by bio-chemistry,
but this is just a small "detail". From a computational point of view, this
shows that the whole theory of computation can be reformulated in terms
of splicing (cutting two strings in two parts each and crossingover, gluing
together the prefix of the first string with the suffix of the second string
and the prefix of the second string with the suffix of the first one), that
rewriting, i.e. local substitutions in a string, as used in all classic computing
models, Turing machines, Markov algorithms, Chomsky grammars, Post
systems, and so on, can be replaced by the much different cut-and-paste
operation. The discussion can be prolonged — I conclude it with mentioning
that my enthusiasm for splicing was so high that in a survey-paper that
I have written for the *Bulletin of the European Association for Theoretical
Computer Science* I have forecasted that *H* systems will become similarly
popular as *L* systems (with *L* coming from "Lindenmayer"), three decades
before. The paper appeared in the formal language column of the *Bulletin*,
at the invitation of Arto; wise enough, he added a note at the end of the
paper, saying something like "this will happen only if *H* systems will have
similarly good applications as *L* systems". At least up to now, Arto was
right: DNA computing has lost a good part of its initial attraction, because,
more than a decade after Adleman's experiment, no real-life computation
was reported.

    This long detour through DNA computing has the point especially
in the last phrase above: after the initial years of hot enthusiasm, many
researchers were looking without success for a "killer-app" and started to
be disappointed with the possibility of using DNA computing for practical
purposes. The main difficulty was related to the errors and the passage
from toy problems to problems of real-life size. The idea was formulated
several times that we have to look closer to what happens *in vivo*, maybe
to implement DNA computations in the natural framework where DNA
evolves, in the cell.

I am sure, now, *a posteriori*, that this idea of looking to the cell in order to implement DNA computations was the one of the unconscious triggers of coming to the idea of membrane computing.

Another trigger, again unconscious (the psychologists will probably say that it always happens in this manner), was a paper presented by Vincenzo Manca (at that time, from Pisa, now from Verona, Italy), at a workshop on DNA computing that I have organized in Mangalia, Romania, in 1997 (it was the first of this kind in Europe, one week before a similar meeting which was organized in Turku, Finland; Tom Head has participated in both of them). The title of the paper was "String rewriting and metabolism: A logical perspective"; the investigation is conducted in terms of logics, but there is a notion, that of *metabolite*, which looks now very much like a ... *P* system.

1.2. *The first years*

It was in October 1998, in Turku, when I came to the explicit idea of defining a computing model inspired from the structure and the functioning of a cell. Membranes enclosing "protected reactors", where chemicals swimming in water react according to given rules (pale reminiscences of the biology I have learned in high school ...); because the multiplicity of chemicals matter (pale reminiscence of the chemistry I learned in high school ...), multisets in the compartments of the device. Rules used in parallel, transitions among configurations, computations. I called the machinery a *super-cell*, because of the generality — in particular, in what concerns the number of levels of hierarchically arranged membranes. A bad name, of course. A lucky mis-inspiration: because people did not like this term, they have used to the one now used — *P* systems.

The first person to propose this name was Kamala Krithivasan, from Madras, India. After having the main definitions and the first results, including universality theorems, I felt that there is "something" here. The flexibility of the model was obvious. Symbol-objects, string-objects; multisets or usual sets; multiset rewriting rules for symbol-objects, string rewriting rules for string-objects. Also, splicing rules for processing string-objects, which directly makes (part of) DNA computing part of membrane computing. Universality, as well as the possibility of defining restricted classes. Visibly, a lot of work to be done. With automata, languages, grammars and complexity connections — which is always good, because many people know automata, languages, grammars and complexity and they are eager to apply what they know in a new area, especially, if this new area is related to biology, a fashion in science in the last decades. I felt scientifically thrilled, much more than in other situations. I wanted to make as soon as possible known the idea, also in order to check whether it is really new or not, and to this aim, I have sent the file of the paper to several friends and collaborators, from many countries. Very few answered — yes, interesting, well, it seems nice, let us see — with Kamala being super-positive, predicting that the devices I have proposed will be called soon P systems. I do not remember now which was the first paper using this term and which were its authors, a fact is that the "super-cells" were used in very few papers and after that the current terminology won.

I was sometimes asked what P from "P system" means, and my favorite answer was "it comes from promising"; with the continuation that, "if somebody will find that these systems are not promising, (s)he may call them non-promising, in short, NP systems, and in this way we will have a first case where $P = NP$". In some papers, some authors explain that P comes from Păun, in a few papers, one even writes, "Păun systems", but there are also papers where one looks for original explanations; I have recently seen a paper where P comes from "priority"!

But, enough with the name, let us go back to the first proofs. As usual, when defining a new model/device/whatever, at the beginning there is no known technique to handle it, and in most cases, the first results are not obtained with the most efficient tools. The first universality theorem for P systems was based on computing polynomials, using the Robinson–Davis–Matijasevich characterization of recursively enumerable sets of numbers, as sets of positive values of polynomials with integer coefficients. Impressive proof — unfortunately, non-necessarily impressive. Just after completing the proof, I have realized that a much simpler one can be obtained starting from the characterization of recursively enumerable languages by means of matrix grammars (of the form mentioned in the previous section). In this form, the paper was circulated among friends, in this form it has appeared already in November 1998 as a technical report of Turku Center for Computer Science, TUCS (Report 208) [5].

At that time, it was a real "Romanian invasion" at TUCS — "old" researchers as me and Sandu, a series of PhD students, short-term visitors. Among the PhD students, Lucian Ilie, now at the same University of Western Ontario, London, Canada, as Lila Kari. Some years later, he remembered to me that in a discussion on the corridor at TUCS, I (was so trustful in the fate of membrane computing that I) predicted that in a few years I will organize an international meeting about this subject, and that he was skeptical about this. I have forgotten this discussion, so for sure the first Workshop on Membrane Computing, Curtea de Argeş, Romania, August 2000, was not organized in order to prove Lucian that he was too skeptical.

Actually, the name of the first meeting was "Workshop on Multiset Processing", on the one hand, because I wanted to start "from the foundations", being somewhat uneasy with what was known before about handling multisets, on the other hand, because I was not sure that a five-days workshop can be organized on the basis only of membrane computing papers. I succeeded to bring in Curtea de Argeş many people who have worked with multisets before, in particular, Jean-Pierre Banâtre, who had introduced already in 1986, together with Daniel Le Métayer, the so-called gamma language (multiset processing by means of chemically inspired rules — of a rather general form and without using compartments, hence membranes). In this context, I have also learned about the chemical abstract machine (CHAM), of Gérard Berry and Gérard Boudol, where membranes and multisets play a central role — but the approach is totally different, based on process algebra and interest in modeling concurrent processes.

The interest for membrane computing has grown unexpectedly fast, so that the workshop from 2001 was explicitly called "on embrane computing", and the name remained the same until now. The 2001 and 2002 editions took place again in Curtea de Argeş, Romania, but from 2003, the meeting was organized every year in another country: Tarragona, Spain, in 2003; Milano, Italy, in 2004; Vienna, Austria, in 2005; Leiden, The Netherlands, in 2006 (with the plans to have it in Thessaloniki, Greece, in 2007, in England in 2008, and back to Curtea de Argeş in 2009, at the tenth edition). It was at the second workshop when Solomon Marcus launched a nice "definition" of life, in the form of the slogan-equation "Life = DNA software + membrane hardware".

Coming back to the initial paper: I have submitted it at the beginning of 1999 to *Journal of Computer and System Sciences*, and in about four months ("Received January 13, 1999; revised June 30, 1999") I got the referee reports as Positive enough. The paper appeared in 2000, after counting already some dozens of titles in the area, that is why the paper both uses the term "P system" and ends with a bibliography containing many titles which were not mentioned in its first version. In February 2003, Thomson Institute for Scientific Information, ISI, nominated it as "fast breaking paper" (see http://esi-topics.com/fbp/fbp-february2003.html).

By this time, already the membrane computing community was much developed, especially at the mathematical level. In 2001, the first PhD thesis in this area was presented: S. N. Krishna, on *Languages of P Systems. Computability and Complexity*, IIT Madras, India. Also in 2001, the web site in Ref. 7 was organized — it is now the most comprehensive source of information on membrane computing. In 2000, I have introduced the so-called *P* systems with active membranes, having rules for dividing membranes; this makes possible the generation of an exponential workspace in a linear number of steps, and in this way, by trading space for time, in this framework we can solve *NP*-complete problems in linear time. This is a very active area of research in this moment. In 2002, I have published a first monograph [6], again with Springer-Verlag. It was maybe too early to write a monograph, but it turned out to be very beneficial for the field, as the book has unified the notation and systematized the stuff — including the problems open at that time and looking of interest to me. (Several of them have been solved in the meantime, so that a possible second edition of the book would now look much different.)

1.3. *The recent years*

Let me consider "recent" the period after introducing in membrane computing the idea of symport/antiport. Initially, it was only intuitive that starting with multisets of objects placed in the compartments defined by a cell-like arrangement of membranes and *only moving objects across membranes* we can compute. Computing by communicating objects, not by changing them, creating, deleting etc. Purely conservative. I have formulated the question of find a way to formalize this intuition to several collaborators, but without having any answer.

The solution arose during the second Workshop on Membrane Computing, where Ioan I. Ardelean, a biologist working for the Institute of Biology of the Romanian Academy, Bucharest (by the way: I have met him at a bureaucratic meeting, where I have abruptly asked him whether he would be interested in listening some details of membrane computing and he immediately got involved in this matter; a rare situation where the participation in a bureaucratic meeting was scientifically useful to me), had an invited talk about the biology of the membrane, and he presented two beautiful processes, those of symport and antiport (two chemicals pass together through the same protein channel, in the same direction in the case of symport and in opposite directions in the case of antiport). Only in the bus towards Bran Castle (for tourists, having a direct connection with Dracula...), in the tourist day of the workshop, in a discussion with my son, Andrei already "intoxicated" by membrane computing, I had the revelation: that's it! So simple, so elegant, fully biological! In the next days, we have proved that, indeed, using symport and antiport rules we can reach again the power of Turing machines.

This idea, together with the idea of active membranes (of involving membranes in the evolution rules, more generally, to make evolve also the membrane structure, not only the multisets from its compartments), have diversified very much the landscape. Indeed, a small jungle of classes of P systems is now studied in the literature. This should not be a surprise, because membrane computing has motivations coming from several contradictory directions: biologists want to have as realistic as possible models (hence full of real-biology aspects), mathematicians want to have as elegant as possible models (hence as restrictive as possible), the computer scientists want to have as powerful (in comparison with Turing machines) and as efficient as possible models (solving computationally hard problems in a feasible time, e.g. by space-time trade-off).

In the meantime, there started to appear applications. At the beginning, as it is natural, in biology. Among the first, T. Y. Nishida, studying photosynthesis; Yasuhiro Suzuki and his collaborators, studying populations in ecosystems; Krishna, Krithivasan, Rama, with (hypothetical) applications in cryptography. Then many others: I. I. Ardelean, in collaboration with Matteo Cavaliere or Daniela Besozzi; Vincenzo Manca and his strong group from Verona; Claudio Zandron (the second holder of a PhD in membrane computing), Giancarlo Mauri, Alberto Leporati and their collaborators from Milan, Italy; Marian Gheorghe, a Romanian who moved to Sheffield, UK, especially interested in quorum sensing in bacteria, hence in tissue-like P systems, not cell-like; Sevilla group, in Spain, led by Mario J. Pérez-Jiménez, with rather elaborated applications in biology/medicine (and major contributions to complexity issues); A. Păun, at Louisiana Tech, Ruston, USA; G. Rozenberg and his group from Leiden, The Netherlands. And others, to whom I apologize not to mention them now.

In 2003, I started a second series of meetings devoted to membrane computing, of a kind not very usual in (modern) science and of which I am very proud to came to idea of organizing: some kind of workshops with emphasis on *work*, with only a few ("provocative") presentations, without any submission of papers and no program (committee); one week for working together. Because everything should have a name, I called it Brainstorming Week on Membrane Computing. Tarragona 2003, Sevilla 2004, 2005, 2006, and probably Sevilla also in the next years. The intention was to have 10–15 researchers together, the result was around 30 in the first year and around 45 in the next years. Incredibly efficient. People free of any duty, just spending the time cooperating with other people from the same area. Large volumes with papers emerged from these meetings were edited each year — see details in the web page [7].

In the third Brainstorming, participated also by a Luca Cardelli, who initiated a series of "brane calculi" (with "brane" coming from "membrane") interested only in processes based on membrane operations (and process algebra issues). The bridge of membrane computing with brane calculi is now an intensive direction of research — for instance, a workshop was devoted to this topic during ICALP 2006, Venice, Italy. This bridge is of interest also in view of the fact that the Microsoft company — with which Luca is associated, is more and more involved in computational biology and systems biology: in December 2005, a Centre for Computational and Systems Biology was founded in Trento, Italy, in collaboration with the local university (my former PhD student, Matteo Cavaliere got a position in that center and started a good cooperation with colleagues coming from process algebra).

Other names of the area? The list of authors of P papers from Ref. 7 is rather long, so I will only mention a very few: Dragoş Sburlan, who, like Matteo Cavaliere started the PhD with me in Tarragona and, when I moved to Sevilla, he also moved here (he is teaching now in Constanţa University, Romania). Artiom Alhazov, from Chişinău, Moldova (the most active participant in any workshop or brainstorming, always having a question to formulate or a new open problem after having settled a problem). Oscar H. Ibarra and his super-efficient group from Santa Barbara, California, USA (Oscar settled several basic open problems of membrane computing: there are classes of P systems with infinite hierarchies on the number of membranes; the deterministic catalytic P systems used in the accepting mode are not universal; one can characterize context-sensitive languages in terms of P systems with symport/antiport etc.). Petr Sosik, from Opava, Czech Republic, always coming with surprising results (catalytic P systems are universal, P systems with active membranes allowed to divide non-elementary membranes characterize **PSPACE**). Serghei Verlan, France, and Pierluigi Frisco, The Netherlands and then

England, who clarified many issues related to P systems with string-objects processed by splicing rules. The Indian groups, centered around Kamala Krithivasan and R. Rama, the Romanian groups (especially of Gabriel Ciobanu, from Iaşi and Timişoara). Yurii Rogozhin (Moldova), Maurice Margenstern (France), Natasha Jonoska (USA), Erzsébet Csuhaj-Varjú and György Vaszil (Hungary), Rudi Freund and his group from Vienna, Linqiang Pan and Haiming Chen (China), Natalio Krasnogor (England), all those mentioned in the previous pages and many others who I do not recall now.

1.4. *The next years*

Well, the past is hard to remember, the present is hard to understand, the future is hard to predict.

Still, I can safely say that membrane computing will continue to be active for a while at least because at this moment it is still growing.

For instance, a very recent and fruitful idea is that of spiking neural P systems, incorporating ingredients from "neural computing of the third generation", that dealing with spiking neurons — these systems were introduced in Ref. 4; and further details can be found in Ref. 7.

Then, membrane computing passes "Salomaa criterion", having applications (at least as many and at least as convincing as L systems). The big stack is related to applications in biology and medicine. The discussion can be longer. Biology needs models and simulation tools; after completing the genome project, the main challenge for bio-informatics is to model and simulate the cell as a whole. The cell is small in size but too complex for the current models, based on differential equations. Differential equations, continuous mathematics, in general, cannot handle processes with a small number of agents/molecules/reactants. Exactly, this is what membrane computing is doing. And it starts from a biological intuition, explicitly taking the cell as a whole as its inspiration. Then, membrane computing models are distributed, easily scalable, understandable, and programmable, can cope with small populations of molecules and with slow reactions (none of these features is shared with models based on differential equations).

Moreover, the range of applications was recently enlarged with two rather promising directions: applications in economics, and in approximate optimization. Economy is the same as biology (discrete, dealing with multisets, in compartments etc.), with a "small" difference: in economy, the "atoms" think (it is attributed to M. Gell-Mann, "the man with five brains", the phrase "Imagine that electrons could think"), and this makes some difference in the kind of models one can use in approaching economic processes. Recent papers by collaborators of Adam Obtulowicz, from Warsaw, Poland, and of Radu Păun (no coincidence of name: he is my second son, now completing a PhD in economics at Maryland, USA) indicate however that this is a worth-pursuing direction of research. Similarly with the "membrane algorithms" proposed in 2004 by T. Y. Nishida: a sort of distributed evolutionary algorithms organized in form of P systems, and proving to be rather efficient (rapidly convergent, in many cases giving the optimal solution, in many cases having the worst and the average solutions better than those provided by other methods etc.).

Whether or not *multiset rewriting in a cell-like membrane structure*, that is, very shortly membrane computing, will sometime become a folklore technique in biology and economics, in the same way as today differential equations are in physics, astronomy, meteorology and other areas, is a question to be checked after, say, some decades. Let me only close these historical notes with the optimistic forecast that this will be the case, and let us pass now to a more technical (though informal) discussion of membrane computing.

2. Elements of Membrane Computing

Of course, this is a very short introduction to membrane computing, only pointing a few basic notions and only presenting some (types of) results and of applications. The reader interested in details should consult [2, 6], and the comprehensive bibliography from Ref. 7. To keep the text shorter, I will not indicate the place where each notion was first introduced, and, moreover, the presentation is not chronological. Such information can be found in the three places just mentioned.

2.1. *The three main classes of P systems*

The field started by looking to the cell in order to learn something possibly useful to computer science, but then the research also considered cell organization in tissues (in general, populations of cells, such as colonies of bacteria), and, recently, also neurons organization in brain. Thus, there are in this moment three main types of P systems: (i) cell-like P systems; (ii) tissue-like P systems and (iii) neural-like P systems.

The first type imitates the (eukaryotic) cell, and its basic ingredient is the *membrane structure*, a hierarchical arrangement of membranes (understood as three dimensional vesicles), delimiting compartments where multisets of symbol objects are placed; rules for evolving these multisets as well as the membranes are provided, also localized, acting in specified compartments or on specified membranes. The objects not only evolve, but they also pass through membranes (we say that they are "communicated" among compartments). The rules can have several forms, and their use can be controlled in various ways: promoters, inhibitors, priorities, etc.

In tissue-like *P* systems, several one-membrane cells are considered as evolving in a common environment. They contain multisets of objects, while also the environment contains objects. Certain cells can communicate directly (channels are provided between them), but all cells can communicate through the environment. The channels can be given in advance or they can be dynamically established — this latter case appears in so-called *population P systems*.

Finally, there are two types of neural-like *P* systems. One of them are similar to tissue-like *P* systems in the fact that the cells (neurons) are placed in the nodes of an arbitrary graph and they contain multisets of objects, but they also have a *state* which controls the evolution. A more promising device was recently introduced in Ref. 4, under the name of *spiking neural P systems*, where one uses only one type of object, the *spike*, and the main information one works with is the distance between consecutive spikes.

The cell-like *P* systems were introduced first and their theory is now very well developed; tissue-like *P* systems have also attracted a considerable interest, while the neural-like systems, mainly under the form of spiking neural *P* systems, are only recently investigated. Applications were reported so far only for the first two classes of *P* systems, the cell-like and the tissue-like ones.

In what follows, in order to let the reader having a flavor of membrane computing, I will discuss in some details only cell-like *P* systems and refer to the area literature for other classes.

2.2. *Cell-like P systems: An informal presentation*

Because from now on I only consider cell-like *P* systems, I will simply call them as *P* systems.

In short, such a system consists of a hierarchical arrangement of *membranes*, which delimit *compartments*, where *multisets* (sets with multiplicities associated with their elements) of abstract *objects* are placed. These objects correspond to the chemicals from the compartments of a cell; the chemicals swim in water (many of them are bound on membranes, but we do not consider this case here, although it started recently to be investigated), and their multiplicity matters — that is why the data structure most adequate to this situation is the multiset (a multiset can be seen as a string modulo permutation, that is why in membrane computing one usually represents the multisets by strings). In what follows, I consider the objects unstructured, hence, I represent them by symbols from a given alphabet.

The objects evolve according to *rules* which are also associated with the regions. The rules say both how the objects are changed and how they can be moved (*communicated*) across membranes. There also are rules which only move objects across membranes, as well as rules for evolving the membranes themselves (e.g. by destroying, creating, dividing, merging membranes). By using these rules, we can change the *configuration* of a system (the multisets from its compartments as well as the membrane structure); we say that we get a *transition* among system configurations.

The rules can be applied in many ways. The basic mode imitates the biological way the chemical reactions are performed — in parallel, with the mathematical additional restriction to have a *maximal parallelism*: one applies a bunch of rules which is maximal, no further object can evolve at the same time by any rule. Besides this mode, there were considered several others: sequential (one rule is used in each step), bounded parallelism (the number of membranes to evolve and/or the number of rules to be used in any step is bounded in advance), minimal parallelism (in each compartment where a rule can be used at least one rule is used). In all cases, a common feature is that the objects to evolve and the rules by which they evolve are chosen in a *non-deterministic* manner. A sequence of transitions forms a *computation* and with computations which *halt* (reach a configuration where no rule is applicable) we associate a *result*, for instance, in the form of the multiset of objects present in the halting configuration in a specified membrane.

This way of using a P system, starting from an initial configuration and computing a number, is a grammar-like (generative) one. We can also work in an automata style: an input is introduced in the system, for instance, in the form of a number represented by the multiplicity of an object placed in a specified membrane, and we start computing; the input number is accepted if and only if the computation halts. A combination of the two modes leads to a functional behavior: an input is introduced in the system (at the beginning, or symbol by symbol during the computation) and also an output is produced. In particular, we can have a decidability case, where the input encodes a decision problem and the output is one of two special objects representing the answers yes and no to the problem.

Thus, we can address several types of problems in this framework. The main two concerns the computing power of P systems (working in the generative or accepting modes), and their usefulness in solving decision problems (making use of the inherent parallelism, it is expected that fast solutions to problems which are hard to solve by sequential algorithms can be found). From both these two points of view, the results are quite attractive: P systems with simple ingredients (number of membranes, forms and sizes of rules, controls of using the rules) are Turing complete, while classes of P systems with enhanced parallelism (e.g. having rules for membrane division) can provide polynomial solutions to **NP**-complete (even **PSPACE**-complete) problems.

The generality of this approach is obvious. We start from the cell, but the abstract model deals with very general notions: membranes interpreted as separators of regions with filtering capabilities, objects and rules assigned to regions; the basic data structure is the multiset. Thus, membrane computing can be interpreted as a *bio-inspired framework for distributed parallel processing of multisets*.

2.3. *Basic ingredients of P systems*

Let us now go into some more specific details — still remaining at an informal level.

As said above, we look to the cell structure and functioning, trying to get suggestions for an abstract computing model. The fundamental feature of a cell is its compartmentalization through membranes. The membranes both define protected "reactors", where specific biochemical reactions take place (starting with the cell membrane which delimit and protect the cell from the environment), and contain proteins which catalyze reactions and, through protein channels, ensure the passage of chemicals from a compartment of the cell to another compartment, as well as the communication with the environment. Thus, the main ingredient of a P system is the *membrane structure*, a hierarchical arrangement of membranes, which delimit compartments; in these compartments, there are

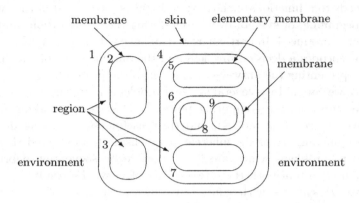

Fig. 2.1.   A membrane structure.

objects, which evolve by means of rules which are also localized, assigned to compartments.

A large variety of P systems can be obtained based on the form of rules and the way they are used, but the membrane structure is common to all cell-like P systems. A suggestive representation of this notion is as in Fig. 2.1. We distinguish the external membrane (corresponding to the plasma membrane and usually called the *skin* membrane) and several internal membranes; a membrane without any other membrane inside it is said to be *elementary*. Each membrane determines a compartment, also called *region*, the space delimited from above by it and from below by the membranes placed directly inside, if any exists. The correspondence membrane-region is one-to-one, so that we identify by the same label a membrane and its associated region.

In the basic class of P systems, each region contains a multiset of symbol-objects, described by symbols from a given alphabet.

The objects evolve by means of evolution rules, which are also localized, associated with the regions of the membrane structure. The typical form of such a rule is $cd \rightarrow (a, here)(b, out)(b, in)$, with the following meaning: one copy of object c and one copy of object d react and the reaction produces one copy of a and two copies of b; the newly produced copy of a remains in the same region (indication *here*), one of the copies of b exits the compartment, going to the surrounding region (indication *out*) and the other enters one of the directly inner membranes (indication *in*). We say that the objects a, b, b are *communicated* as indicated by the commands associated with them in the right-hand member of the rule. When an object exits the skin membrane, it is "lost" in the environment, it never comes back into the system. If no inner membrane exists (that is, the rule is associated with an elementary membrane), then the indication *in* cannot be followed, and the rule cannot be applied.

A rule as above, with several objects in its left-hand member, is said to be *cooperative*; a particular case is that of *catalytic* rules, of the form $ca \rightarrow cx$, where a is an object and c is a catalyst, appearing only in such rules, never changing. A rule of the form $a \rightarrow x$, where a is an object, is called *non-cooperative*.

The rules associated with a compartment are applied to the objects from that compartment. The most investigated way to use the rules is the *maximally parallel one*: all objects which can evolve by means of local rules should do it (we assign objects to rules, until no further assignment is possible). The used objects are "consumed", the newly produced objects are placed in the compartments of the membrane structure according to the communication commands assigned to them. The rules to be used and the objects to evolve are chosen in a non-deterministic manner. In turn, all compartments of the system evolve at the same time, synchronously (a common clock is assumed for all membranes). Thus, we have two layers of parallelism, one at the level of compartments and one at the level of the whole "cell".

Note that evolution rules are stated in terms of *names of objects*, they are "multiset rewriting rules", while their application/execution is done using *copies of objects*.

A membrane structure and the multisets of objects from its compartments identify a *configuration* of a P system. By a non-deterministic maximally parallel use of rules as suggested above we pass to another configuration; such a step is called a *transition*. A sequence of transitions constitutes a *computation*. A computation is successful if it halts, it reaches a configuration where no rule can be applied to the existing objects. With a halting computation we can associate a *result* in various ways. The simplest possibility is to count the objects present in the halting configuration in a specified elementary membrane; this is called *internal output*. We can also count the objects which leave the system during the computation, and this is called *external output*. In both cases the result is a number. If we distinguish among different objects, then we can have as the result a vector of natural numbers. The objects which leave the system can also be arranged in a sequence according to the moments when they exit the skin membrane, and in this case the result is a string.

Because of the non-determinism of the application of rules, starting from an initial configuration, we can get several successful computations, hence several results. Thus, a P system *computes* (one also uses to say *generates*) a set of numbers, or a set of vectors of numbers, or a language.

As mentioned in the previous section, a P system can also be used in the accepting mode, with a particular case being that of solving decision problems, which will be discussed further in Section 2.6.

2.4. *A large number of variants*

Let us start by considering the possibility offered by the form of rules. In the systems described above, the symbol objects were processed by multiset rewriting-like rules (some objects are transformed into other objects, which have associated communication targets). Coming closer to the trans-membrane transfer of molecules, we can consider rules which model the active passage of chemicals through membranes, by so-called *uniport, symport,* and *antiport* (see Ref. 1 for details). Symport refers to the transport where two (or more) molecules pass together through a membrane in the same direction, antiport refers to the transport where two (or more) molecules pass through a membrane simultaneously, but in opposite directions, while the case when a molecule does not need a "partner" for a passage is referred to as uniport.

In mathematical terms, we can consider object processing rules of the following forms: a symport rule (associated with a membrane i) is of the form (ab, in) or (ab, out), stating that the objects a and b enter/exit together membrane i, while an antiport rule is of the form $(a, out; b, in)$, stating that, simultaneously, a exits and b enters membrane i; uniport corresponds to a particular case of symport rules, of the form $(a, in), (a, out)$. An obvious generalization is to consider symport rules (x, in), (x, out) and antiport rules $(x, out; y, in)$ with x, y arbitrary multisets of objects.

Symport/antiport rules can be used alone, thus leading to symport/antiport P systems, or in combination with multiset rewriting rules. In the first case, because by communication we do not create new objects, we need a supply of objects in the environment, otherwise we are only able to handle a finite population of objects, those provided in the initial multisets. Thus, the environment takes an active part in the computation, which is an attractive feature of this class of P systems, together with the conservation of objects, the mathematical elegance, the computational power, the direct biological inspiration. Also the case of evolving objects by means of multiset rewriting rules and communicating by symport/antiport rules leads to a rather interesting class of P systems, the so-called evolution-communication P systems.

A more general form of rules, covering both multiset rewriting and symport/antiport rules, is that of *boundary rules*: $u[_i v \rightarrow u'[_i v'$, where u, v are multisets of objects and i is a membrane, specifies the fact that the multiset u placed outside membrane i and multiset v placed inside membrane i evolve simultaneously into multisets u', v', respectively. Such rules are very powerful, because they have a high degree of context-sensitivity.

Recently, efforts are made to also take into considerations the fact that the cell biochemistry is controlled in a large extent by the proteins embedded in the membranes. For instance, rules of the form $a[_i p|b \rightarrow a'[_i p'|b'$ are proposed, where a, a', b, b' are objects, p, p' are proteins, and $[_i p|$ is a notation of the fact that p is placed on membrane i; several restrictions can be considered, for instance, with $p = p'$, and/or $a = b', b = a'$, etc.

We can then pass to rules which handle not only objects, but also membranes. There is a large list of suggestions coming from biology: membranes can be broken (and the contents remains free in the surrounding region), divided (with the replication of the contents), their contents can be merged or separated according to given criteria; then, there are operations like exocytosis and endocytosis/phagocytosis, budding, matting, gemmating (sending vesicles at specified destinations), and so on and so forth. These last rules ensure that not only the multisets of objects evolve, but also the membrane structure of a P system.

Many possibilities arise in what concerns the way the rules are used. More precisely, the non-determinism of choosing the rules to apply can be decreased in various ways: using a priority among rules (a partial order relation), using promoters (objects which should be present in order to apply a rule) or inhibitors (objects which should not be present), controlling the permeability of membranes (some rules can increase the permeability of the membrane where they are used, other rules can decrease the permeability; a rule which asks for sending an object across a membrane which is not permeable cannot be applied, and in this way the rules can influence the way the next rules are chosen).

Then, we can use the rules in the maximally parallel manner, but also in other ways: sequentially (one rule in the whole system, or in each region), with a bounded parallelism (at least k or exactly k rules in the whole system or in each region), with a minimal parallelism (at least one rule is used in each region where a rule can be used). These strategies of applying the rules are biologically inspired but mathematically oriented; when using P systems as models of biological systems/processes, we have to use more realistic features, in general, of a numerical nature (e.g. reaction rates, probabilities), computed dynamically, depending on the current population of objects in the system.

I do not give here a formal definition of a P system. The reader interested in mathematical and bibliographical details can consult the mentioned monograph [6], as well as the relevant papers from Ref. 7. Of course, when presenting a P system we have to specify: the alphabet of objects (a usual finite non-empty alphabet of abstract symbols identifying the objects), the membrane structure (usually represented by a string of labeled matching parentheses), the multisets of objects present in each region of the system (represented by strings of symbol-objects), the sets of evolution rules associated with each region, possibly also the priority relation for each set of rules, as well as the indication about the way the output is defined. In the case of symport/antiport systems, also the objects available in the environment should be specified.

2.5. *Computational completeness*

As we have mentioned before, many classes of P systems, combining various ingredients (as described above or similar) are able of simulating Turing machines, hence they are *computationally complete*. Always, the proofs of results of this type are constructive, and this has an important consequence from the computability point of view: there are *universal* (hence *programmable*) P systems. In short, starting from a universal Turing machine (or an equivalent universal device), we get an equivalent universal P system. Among others, this implies that in the case of Turing complete classes of P systems, the hierarchy on the number of membranes always collapses (at most at the level of the universal P systems). Actually, the number of membranes sufficient in order to characterize the power of Turing machines by means of P systems is always rather small.

We only mention here three of the most interesting (types of) universality results:

(1) P systems with symbol-objects with catalytic rules, using only two catalysts and two membranes, are computationally universal.

(2) *P* systems with symport/antiport rules of a restricted size (example: three membranes, symport rules of weight 2 and no antiport rules, or three membranes and minimal symport and antiport rules) are universal.

(3) *P* systems with symport/antiport rules (of arbitrary size), using only three membranes and only three objects, are universal.

There are several results similar to those mentioned above, improvements or extensions of them; details can be found in Refs. 3 and 7.

We can conclude that the compartmental computation in a cell-like membrane structure (using various ways of communicating among compartments) is rather powerful. The "computing cell" is a powerful "computer".

Universality results were obtained also in the case of *P* systems working in the accepting mode. An interesting problem appears in this case, because we can consider deterministic systems. Most universalities were obtained in the deterministic case, but there also are situations where the deterministic systems are strictly less powerful than the non-deterministic ones.

The hierarchy on the number of membranes collapses in many cases also for non-universal classes of *P* systems, but there are also cases when the number of membrane matters, and the corresponding hierarchies are infinite.

2.6. *Computational efficiency*

The computational power (the "competence") is only one of the important questions to be dealt with when defining a new (bio-inspired) computing model. The other fundamental question concerns the computing *efficiency*. Because *P* systems are parallel computing devices, it is expected that they can solve hard problems in an efficient manner — and this expectation is confirmed for systems provided with ways for producing an exponential workspace in a linear time. Three main such biologically inspired possibilities have been considered so far in the literature, and *all of them were proven to lead to polynomial — often linear — solutions to* **NP**-*complete problems.*

These three ideas are *membrane division, membrane creation,* and *string replication.* The standard problems addressed in this framework were decidability problems, starting with SAT, the Hamiltonian Path problem, the Node Covering problem, but also other types of problems were considered, such as the problem of inverting one-way functions, or the Subset-sum and the Knapsack problems (note that the last two are numerical problems, where the answer is not of the yes/no type, as in decidability problems).

Roughly speaking, the framework for dealing with complexity matters is that of *accepting P systems with input*: a family of P systems of a given type is constructed starting from a given problem, and an instance of the problem is introduced as an input in such systems; working in a deterministic mode (or a *confluent* mode: some non-determinism is allowed, provided that the branching converges after a while to a unique configuration, or, in the weak confluent case, all computations halt and all of them provide the same result), in a given time one of the answers yes/no is obtained, in the form of specific objects sent to the environment. The family of systems should be constructed in a uniform way by a Turing machine, working a polynomial time.

This direction of research is very active at the present moment. More and more problems are considered, the membrane computing complexity classes are refined, characterizations of the $\mathbf{P} \neq \mathbf{NP}$ conjecture were obtained in this framework, improvements are looked for. Two important recent results in this area are the following.

(1) The family **PSPACE** is equal to $\mathbf{PMC}_D$, the family of problems which can be solved in polynomial time by P systems with the possibility of dividing both elementary and non-elementary membranes. The **PSPACE**-complete problem used in the proof of the inclusion **PSPACE** $\subseteq \mathbf{PMC}_D$ was QSAT.

(2) The family **P**, of problems which can be solved in polynomial time by deterministic Turing machines, is the same with the family of problems which can be solved in polynomial time by P systems with membrane division, without using polarizations, and without using membrane dissolution. The proof cannot be extended to the case when membrane dissolution is used, which points out to a surprising role played in this context by the operation of membrane dissolution, never so far believed to be so powerful (from the efficiency point of view). Furthermore, when both dissolution and division of non-elementary rules are used (but not polarizations), one can solve **NP**-complete problems in polynomial time, which (unless if $\mathbf{P} = \mathbf{NP}$) implies that either dissolution or the fact that one divides non-elementary membranes, or both together, make the difference between efficiency and non-efficiency in this framework.

There are in this area a series of interesting open problems, mainly related to the borderline between efficiency (the possibility to solve computationally hard problems in polynomial time) and non-efficiency. For instance, we know that membrane division is necessary for efficiency. However, all constructions from the proofs of the results mentioned above about P systems using division of elementary membranes use "polarized" membranes, marked with one of the three "electrical charges" $+, -, 0$. It was recently shown that the number of polarizations can be decreased to two, but it is an intriguing open problem whether or not the polarizations can be completely removed. A similar borderline question concerns the characterization of **PSPACE**: the proof uses division of non-elementary membranes, which is a rather powerful operation, because also the inner membranes are replicated; can this be avoided, e.g. solving QSAT in polynomial time by using systems with division of only elementary membranes?

2.7. *Applications*

I have already mentioned a series of applications of membrane computing — and the good features of P systems which make them attractive, especially when devising models for biology.

Actually, the applications reported up to now are developed at various levels. In many cases, what is actually used is the *language* of membrane computing, having in mind the long list of concepts either newly introduced, or related in a new manner in this area, the mathematical formalism, and the graphical language, the way to represent cell-like structures or tissue-like structures, together with the contents of the compartments and the associated evolution rules (the "evolution engine"). However, this level of application/usefulness is only a preliminary, superficial one. The next level is to use tools, techniques, results of membrane computing, and here there appears an important question: to which aim? Solving problems already stated, e.g. by biologists, in other terms and another framework, could be an impressive achievement, and this is the most natural way to proceed — but not necessarily the most efficient one, at least at the beginning. New tools can suggest new problems, which either cannot be formulated in a previous framework (in plain language, as it is the case in biology, whatever specialized the specific jargon is, or using other tools, such as differential equations) or have no chance to be solved in the previous framework.

Applications of all these types were reported in the literature of membrane computing. As expected and as natural, most applications were carried out in biology, but also applications in computer graphics (where the compartmentalization seems to add a significant efficiency to well-known techniques based on L systems), linguistics (both as a representation language for various concepts related to language evolution, dialogue, semantics, and making use of the parallelism, in solving parsing problems in an efficient way), economics, in devising sorting and ranking algorithms, cryptography, approximate algorithms for optimization problems etc.

These applications are usually based on experiments using programs for simulating/implementing P systems on usual computers, and there are already many such programs, more and more elaborated (e.g. with better and better interfaces, which allow for the friendly interaction with the program). I plainly avoid to say that we have "implementations" of P systems, because of the inherent non-determinism and the massive parallelism of the basic model, features which cannot be implemented, at least in principle, on the usual electronic computer — but which can be implemented on a dedicated, re-configurable, hardware, or on a local network, on clusters etc. This does not mean that simulations of P systems on usual computers are not useful; such programs were used in all biological applications mentioned above, and can also have important didactic and research applications.

The scenario of these applications in biology (economics) is the following: one takes a process, especially related to controlling pathways in the cell (interplay of agents, e.g. in a market, respectively), one builds a P system modeling it, then one writes a program for simulating this model or one uses a program available on the Internet; using the program, one runs experiments, changing the initial configuration, changing some rules, tuning certain parameters. The output is in general in the form of diagrams showing the evolution in time of the population of certain objects. In all cases, these diagrams are much similar to the ones suggested by laboratory experiments or by other models, and this proves that the approach is faithful, reliable, the machinery works. Of course, this is only half of the road, this is only "postdiction"; what remains to do is to try *predictions*, working with hypotheses and providing conclusions not know yet from experiments. The things are pretty advanced and such results are expected soon.

Another rather promising direction of application is that proposed recently by T. Y. Nishida: distributed evolutionary computing algorithms using ingredients from membrane computing in organizing the search of good solutions to hard optimization problems. The basic variant of such *evolutionary membrane algorithms* is the following one: a (small) number of candidate solutions to an optimization problem are placed in the regions of a membrane structure of a linear shape (with the membranes embedded one in another one), together with local sub-algorithms which can improve the local solutions; after a (small) number of steps of local work, when the solutions from each membrane are evolved, the best of them is sent to the immediately lower membrane and the worst is sent to the immediately upper membrane (with exceptions to this rule in the innermost and the outermost membrane); in this way, the better solutions are moved down and the worst ones are moved up in the membrane hierarchy; this process is iterated until either a specified number of steps is reached, or no improvement of the best solution is obtained for a specified number of steps. When halting, the central membrane provides the answer, the solution to the problem. There are several variants, in terms of the number of membranes, with the initial solutions generated by a first generation of membrane algorithms (thus working in a two-stage manner, which proves to be very efficient), with the possibility to create or to destroy certain membranes during the computation etc. This strategy was checked both by T. Y. Nishida and other researchers for a variety of problems and the results are rather encouraging. Trusting the cell biology, I am quite optimistic with this type of applications.

References

[1] B. Alberts, A. Johnson, J. Lewis, M. Raff, K. Roberts and P. Walter, *Molecular Biology of the Cell*, 4th edn. (Garland Science, New York, 2002).

[2] G. Ciobanu, Gh. Păun and M. J. Pérez-Jiménez, eds., *Applications of Membrane Computing* (Springer, Berlin, 2005).

[3] R. Freund, Gh. Păun, G. Rozenberg and A. Salomaa, eds., *Membrane Computing 6th International Workshop, WMC6, Vienna, Austria, July 2005, Revised Selected and Invited Papers*, LNCS 3859, Springer, Berlin, 2006.

[4] M. Ionescu, Gh. Păun and T. Yokomori, Spiking neural P systems, *Fundamenta Informaticae* **71**(2–3) (2006) 279–308.

[5] Gh. Păun, Computing with membranes, *J. Comput. Syst. Sci.* **61**(1) (2000) 108–143 (and Turku Center for Computer Science-TUCS Report 208, November 1998, www.tucs.fi).

[6] Gh. Păun, *Membrane Computing: An Introduction* (Springer, Berlin, 2002).

[7] The Web Page of Membrane Computing: http://psystems.disco.unimib.it.

Chapter 3

CRITIQUE OF COMPUTATIONAL REASON IN THE NATURAL SCIENCES*

GIUSEPPE LONGO

Département d'Informatique
CNRS — Ecole Normale Supérieure and CREA,
Ecole Polytechnique, Paris
longo@di.ens.fr
http://www.di.ens.fr/users/longo/

In this text, we attempt to shortly highlight certain constitutive principles of the particular form of knowledge provided by the digital machine, the modern computer, in its relationship to mathematics (from which it originates) and to the natural sciences (physics and biology). Our basic thesis is that the historical and conceptual richness of the theory which enabled the concrete realization of this extraordinary type of machine is far from being neutral or transparent with regard to reality. Specifically, we will see that the digital machine proposes causal structures and the breakings of symmetry which are intrinsic to its theory as being the central structures of the intelligibility of nature. This will enable to point out a distinction between "imitation" and "modeling" in terms of simulation or formalization, and therefore enable to highlight the limits and the potentialities of digital simulation.

1. From the Alphabet to the Machine

The extraordinary innovation to which we are confronted today is a machine which is the result of a very specific historical evolution. This machine did not exist "before", in the way in which there were no mammals on earth 300 million years ago. It is within the evolutive system's dynamics, which constantly produces novelty, that mammals emerge: nothing miraculous,

---

*Text originally written in Italian as *Lezione Galileana*, Pisa, 25 Ottobre 2006, in Pianeta Galileo, 2007. A French version is also downloadable at: *http://www.di.ens.fr/users/longo*.

only a very complex mixture between invariance and variability, continuity and change, which are in part random, and in part not yet properly classifiable into current physical categories of determination. In a similar or more complex fashion, human history develops, and within it, with a continuity/discontinuity which is rich in terms of common practices, of language, and of symbolic culture, we invented this machine, which is in the process of changing the world. Such a machine is the culminating point of a very specific process which begins with language, but which is mainly influenced by the birth and development of the alphabet: the digital machine is at first an alphabetic machine, and then a logical and formal one. In short, it is an invention which is both extraordinary and contingent to our culture, which is marked by the birth of the alphabet, of Cartesian rationality, of Fregean logic, of Hilbertian formalism.

So let us enunciate the problem of considering what is the impact of such a machine on the construction of knowledge. The machine is indeed not neutral; it imposes upon one who uses it a history and a logic, an organizing view of phenomena. The most deleterious cultural attitudes are of those who remain naive before the novelty brought on by evolution and history (or that we bring into it): not knowing how to live according to our own knowledge, not knowing how to appreciate the originality of our own knowledge, and projecting our latest invention onto the past, as if, while rich in human history, it was already in the world, or if it were an accurate image of it. And continuing to say: the universe is a big computer, or ... each physical or biological process is a computation. Or that Turing's theory is "complete" and "maximal": even a cell's activity or quantum computing can be reduced to it. This is a pretense to having the "Definitive theory", in an Aristotelian sense.

And, most of all, we do not consider the originality of this extraordinary science and of this technology which, by organizing our view upon phenomena in their own way (and in their own image), help and *guide* us in the acquisition of knowledge. The machine, as other instruments in the past did and even more so, deeply impacts our relationship to science, as the alphabet and the printing press have transformed and impacted our societies, even the way in which we construct knowledge. I will not dwell on all the themes we have evoked, and I will only point out the view which computer science proposes, one imbued by a very effective organization of knowledge into little boxes, into bits, into pixels, into a discrete or sometimes absolute exactitude, with no smoothness, no fuzziness, no gestalt and no alea. Or with at best some very important imitations (in a sense to be specified below) of such components of the world and of knowledge, but ones which are forced or biased by their own logic.

So, I would like to readdress the fact that the roots of this machine are very old and can be found in the alphabet. First of all, 5,000–6,000 years ago, the alphabet was, for different reasons, an invention comparable to the computer-mediated discretization of knowledge we have now performed. Think of the originality of these first social groups from Mesopotamia who fractioned the linguistic flux, a *continuous* spoken song, marking certain pitches as first consonants [12]. It was the onset of a development and of a culture which were quite different to those inherent to the hieroglyphic writing of ideograms which proposed concepts or evoked whole images, situations, or feelings, by means of drawings. Conversely, the alphabet discretizes, subdivides continuous language into insignificant atoms, into the bits which are letters. This constitutes an extraordinary leap of abstraction by man, a way of representing linguistic interaction which absolutely did not exist before and which will mark human culture by the (re-)construction of meaning from elementary and simple signs without meaning, signs that were highly abstract as such. Moreover, and this is crucial, meaning is reconstructed through sound: the alphabet is phonetic. Meaning is provided by the reproduction of sound, and not by the evocation of an image or of a concept, a huge revolution. In computer science terms, the phoneme is the alphabet's compiler, or the "interpreter" if you wish, and it produces meaning. By means of the drawing, hieroglyph or ideogram, the evocation of a concept, of an emotion or of a god is conveyed in silence. The road sign, an ideogram, imposes a direction, an order, or a prohibition in the visual immediateness of a significant evocation: it is understood, acted upon, without the production of sound, not even mental. If on the other hand, for example, the indication which prohibits turning right by means of an evocative sign is written, as is often the case in the USA, you will necessarily pronounce the words "no right turn", at least in thought. Producing a phoneme, one which is exclusively mental when reading in silence, is necessary to obtain meaning, and we all go through the difficulties posed by our first attempts at decryption during childhood, which is necessary performed vocally when learning (it would appear that silent reading was not invented until the IIIrd or IVth century: before that, western man would always read aloud). Musical writing will undergo the same process and an expert musician mentally hears music when reading it, even silently, just as we hear alphabet-based significant words, because they resound.

2. The Elementary and the Complex

With the observations on the alphabet's role, I took up the detailed and profound observations made by Herrenschmidt in Paris, by Sini [21] and his school in Milan, as well as to other authors: alphabetic fractioning will orient human culture in a very strong way. Let us see how and why this has anything to do with computer science.

The alphabet is extraordinarily effective: it forces into shape, it canalizes and organizes thought, and it structures knowledge. First, it introduces an original form of dualism: here, notation, there, signification, linked by means of the phoneme, but also independent (with the ideogram, signification is immanent to the drawing). Then, there is the conception according to which, in order to understand the world, it is necessary to fraction it into *elementary* and *simple* components. Democritus designated atoms by means of the letters of the alphabet: the universe is constructed in the image of our invention, the alphabet, and is formed by the combination of elementary and simple components, which are indivisible, like letters. Today, the genome is still described by means of letters of the alphabet. Atoms, or genome's bases and molecules, aggregate between each other, and then, there emerges, as a pop-out, the physical object, the phenotype, the behavior: just how meaning emerges by aggregation of letters and by means of the phoneme. And man projects, once more, this manner of reconstructing and of talking about the world, onto the absolute: he says that God (or evolution) invented the world and life in the way he constructs meaning himself with alphabetic reading, by juxtaposing signs with no signification. Once more, the alphabet is very effective and extraordinary, but it is not a neutral instrument, it imposes by its own force the paradigms which will be at the origin of western science and which are still re-visited today in contemporary science. Particularly, it proposes the paradigm that Descartes, more than anyone else, placed at the center of knowledge: the elementary components of the construction of knowledge must be very simple, insecable links of the rational chain of Cartesian reasoning. Letters, in themselves, are indecomposable (elementary), are very simple, and do not have meaning, but when arranged together, they produce meaning that can be very complex. Such is Democritus's approach to science, but also, I insist, that of Aristotle and of Descartes: intelligibility is produced by the decomposition of the universe into atoms and the discourse on the universe into *simple* and *elementary* links. It is the maximal, atomic decomposition of elements which makes the universe intelligible and discourse rigorous. This is how Galileo and Newton work and all of modern science, with an incredible effectiveness, constructs knowledge, from the elementary and the simple. It has been more productive than any other science (the Chinese come to mind, for instance) especially for making machines, though not exclusively. Clocks are made like this: they are composed and highly complex objects made from simple gears and belts, in the way XVIIIth century clockmakers would make them. And so is made the computer: the logical gates and elementary components are very simple; programming languages are composed of elementary and simple linguistic atoms, and used to make systems and programs of an extraordinary degree of complexity.

However, we are faced today with an enormous difficulty, a new challenge in terms of knowledge: in the two most innovative fields, at the difficult frontier of knowledge, quantum physics and biology, *the elementary is in fact very complex*, and this is the great challenge to our understanding, with our being so alphabetized. We can refer to the case of strings or to the phenomena of non-separability and non-locality specific to quantum physics which are of an extreme level of complexity and which concern *elementary* components of matter. So, our projection of the alphabet upon the world, the letter-atoms of Democritus, suddenly faces an obstacle, which is for the moment insurmountable (we cannot understand microphysics in classical or relativistic terms). The same thing is happening with the analysis of living phenomena: the cell, as elementary component of living matter (if we split it, it dies; it is no longer living) is very complex, and must be considered in its unity. Some biologists (Gould, among many others) assert that a eukaryotic cell is as complex as an elephant. Indeed, within a cell reside the same proteinic cascades, the same type of energy production (mitochondria, metabolism...), a structuring into organs that is analogous to that which exists in a metazoan. An aspect of complexity, the objective one, is therefore similar in the elephant and in the eukaryotic cell. An animal is obviously more complex than a cell from the phenotypical point of view, but that is another type of complexity (morphological). The new challenge, the complexity of the elementary is a conceptual obstacle to our alphabetic and digital decomposition of the world, which is otherwise very effective: we have difficulties overcoming it. As in quantum physics, where there lacks unity with the classical or relativistic "field", we have trouble unifying the "field" of living phenomena (which we have also not yet defined) with current biochemical theories, the theories which use macromolecules and bases as words and alphabet. A reflection in this regard, thanks to the contribution (by duality) of digital computer science, could possibly help.

3. Imitations and Models

Let us return to the digital. So, it is the strength of alphabetic culture which has given us this machine, the digital computer, as its ultimate expression, the culminating point of human, alphabetic, and Cartesian invention. The machine is alphabetical, above all because everything is composed of 0s and 1s. The basic alphabet is very simple and also has very simple elements, and it then becomes very complex, by composition. It is Cartesian because it is the maximal locus of Cartesian dualism, realized from Turing's idea in 1936: the electrical calculating machines of that era and which continued to be used until the 1950s did not have software that was distinguishable from the hardware. They would have multiplication implemented within them, in a way, and it would remain inscribed in the gears: the rules, one by one, would shape the hardware which was constructed ad hoc. These machines were constructed as were clocks 200 years earlier, only being more complex. Turing's idea, having some predecessors, was to clearly and mathematically distinguish, in the abstract machine, the hardware, as multi-functional physical material, from the software. Then the theory of programming, completely independent from hardware, emerged from specific electronics. The main idea making computer science possible is the portability of software, in its independence from hardware: a program is written, is moved from one machine to another, and it works. It can be sold independently. There exists a line of work which I have practiced for a long time, that of mathematical logician in Programming Theory, and which is completely independent from the analysis of hardware. Naturally, to a monist like myself, this has nothing to do with the world, and even less to do with living phenomena: it is rather the modern image of mind/body Cartesian dualism, with its lot of metempsychosis (the transferal of programs and operating system from a dying computer to another) which enjoys a great success in Artificial Intelligence and in bad sci-fi movies. I do insist, however, that such a paradigm is rich in knowledge, beginning with the construction of the alphabet, may be the first truly dualist experience of man, as we were saying: insignificant sign and signification, each being highly distinguished from the other. And, I would re-call Aristotle once more. He outlines a theory of memory and of reasoning based on the alphabet according to which, he asserts, the unfolding of reasoning is like the marking, the stamping of "alphabetic signs on the body, as on a wax tablet" [10]: it is the alphabetic signs that enable reasoning with their purely formal dynamic which is independent from meaning. Thought resides in the *mobile impression of signs*. This constitutes Aristotle's and Turing's alphabetic model of reasoning (the Turing machine could be called the Aristotle–Turing machine): letters which move and which are impressed upon matter (living matter, as on wax), or on the ribbon of a Turing machine, the prototype of the modern computer. From then on, we get to a machine which represents everything, through Cartesian and atomist reasoning, by means of a sequence of letters without signification. This way of understanding human (and animal) intelligence canalizes the view on reality with great effectiveness, but it is biased, by a bias resulting on the one hand from its dualistic aspects (that I would qualify as ferocious) and on the other hand, from the fact of only proposing intelligibility by means of the reduction to the simple and elementary, the sequence of ultimate and very simple signs/atoms, without meaning. Once more, this paradigm was very rich for (classical) physico-mathematical knowledge and technologies, particularly, but today it remains confronted to the obstacle of this very complex, non-alphabetical elementarity which we find in quantum physics and biology, and which is rich in entanglements and causal circularities specific to these two theoretical frames.

The first consequence to draw from these considerations is an invitation to a lot of circumspection when using the computer as instrument of intelligibility. In other words, it is important to not do like some colleagues, in the natural sciences too, who consider as valid everything they see on the screen, the models which the machine enable. To this day, the richness of the digital simulation is such that it deserves a fine, an epistemological analysis in particular, precisely in order to do better and more.

I would like to note that Turing himself, in this regard, introduced an implicit but fine distinction between "imitation" and "model", with the intuition, after 1948, of an intrinsic limit to his machine which he will qualify as "Laplacian" in the 1950s. To understand what he meant, let us take an example, the double pendulum. It consists in a physical object which is very sensitive to the initial conditions. It may be formalized by two very informative differential equations determining its movements: two rods connected by a pivot, two weights... from the mathematical viewpoint, there are only two variables, one single law, gravitation, and despite that... chaos. From the intelligibility standpoint, those who know non-linear systems will immediately understand that this artifact is very sensitive to initial conditions (the Lyapounov coefficients can tell the mathematician this). If we launch the pendulum from certain initial values, inevitably, within the range of possible physical measurement, and if we then re-launch it, within the same range, that of observability, then a variation, a fluctuation below the observable (or non-measurable, for example thermal fluctuation) suffices to give the double pendulum a completely different course. The double pendulum, a perfectly deterministic machine (it is only determined by two equations!), is sensitive to minor variations, below the threshold of observability: it is a typical chaotic deterministic system, as there are many of them.[1]

On the other hand, when observing digital simulations (an implementation can be found on http://www.mathstat.dal.ca/~selinger/lagrange1/doublependulum.html), we can clearly see dense trajectories: thanks to the simulation, we can make the pendulum oscillate long enough and can observe that it tends to cover all the space of possible trajectories. This is an aspect of chaos. Yet, when we click on "restart" (re-launching the pendulum with the same initial data), it again takes the exact same trajectory. With a real and physical pendulum however, this is absolutely impossible. If we have a good pendulum at hand, one sufficiently insensitive to friction, but a physical pendulum, not a virtual one, then even the thermal fluctuation, which is inherent to the physical process, suffices to launch it upon another trajectory, if re-initialized. Therefore, this excellent imitation which tells us so many very useful things, what does it actually propose? On the one hand, it shows us the density of the trajectories, typical of deterministic chaos, but on the other hand, it causes us to

---

[1]The notion of deterministic chaos is mathematically very solid and is 110 years old (Poincaré), even if its modern definitions date back only to the 1960s and 1970s. These definitions may be summarized as follows: a deterministic physical system (a system considered to be determined or determinable by an evolution function or a finite number of equations, such as a double pendulum, the planetary system, a coin tossed within a gravitational field over a mathematically describable area...) is chaotic when it is "topologically transitive" (there are dense orbits, that is, orbits that go everywhere within the border conditions), when it has a "dense set of periodic points" and is "sensitive to the initial conditions". These properties can be described with mathematical rigor (let us note that such is the case for the three above-mentioned systems: so is the solar system, according to recent results, see [14]. In what concerns images, the attractor of a non-linear system, even in one dimension (an equation, such as $x_{n+1} = 4x_n(1 - x_n)$), truly evokes what Plato would also qualify as chaos (superimposition of lines or points, "creazy" oscillations...). Deterministic chaos is therefore not an oxymoron, despite of some bad vulgarization, but a very solid mathematical notion. As a great instrument of intelligibility, it enables to understand classical randomness, as opposed to quantum randomness, see [4], as a determination which does not imply predictability (nor iterability: a classical process is random when, in general, it does not follow the same "trajectory" despite being iterated with the same initial conditions, within the limit of physical measure); this is the great shift relatively to Laplace's conjecture, according to which "determination implies predictability".

lose an essential piece of information: in a dynamic (non-linear) system, it especially occurs that, once re-initialized, the systems never take the same "trajectory". And this because of "principles" which are inherent to physics (modern physics): physical measurement is always an interval and the (inevitable) variation, below the threshold of measurement, suffices to very quickly produce a different evolution. The analysis of the equations within the *continuum* leads to an understanding of this random aspect of chaos, whereas computational imitation makes it disappear completely, by the discrete nature of its data types. Only tricks and stratagems (pseudo-synchronization with distant watches, pseudo-random generators introduced ad hoc) can imitate, but not modelize, the physical phenomenon. That is, they can deceive the observer of virtual reality, as Turing hopes to deceive the observer in the man/machine/woman *imitation* game, as he called it, but they cannot propose a physico-mathematical "model" of the possible causal structure of the physical phenomenon, as I would like to explain. For those with a physico-mathematical sensitivity, it is almost funny to see a computer simulation in which, by giving the same numeric initial values, a double pendulum, or a turbulence, will take the exact same trajectory, because this makes no physical sense. This is a case of imitation, as Turing would rightfully say. Indeed: this term which I have used in a few articles (downloadable from my web page), has been suggested by Turing who, after 1948, began to take interest in dynamical systems, and stopped asserting that his machine was a huge brain. In 1950, he wrote an article on how to imitate human behavior using his machine [22] (the imitation game between the machine and... a woman: can they be distinguished in a teletype-mediated dialog? Turing had a complex relationship with women and was homosexual). In 1952, though, he published an article on morphogenesis [22] which proposed a very original non-linear system of action-reaction and dynamic diffusion, in which he provided what he called a *model* of the physical phenomenon in question. He thus sought to propose a structure of determination, by means of the equations describing causal interaction in the action-reaction process.

I hope that the implicit distinction to be found in Turing and which I have developed here can be useful to better understand what is done thanks to the digital machine: so I will return to it.

A model (a physico-mathematical one) is an attempt to express a *possible structure of physical causality*. For example, Newton considers movement (of planets and of masses) and writes equations, among which $f = ma$, that make the dynamics intelligible. That is, he makes a formidable proposition, as follows: force causes acceleration, with mass as proportionality coefficient. He proposes, with his equations, a structure of causality which will enable to deduct, among other things, the Kepler orbits. From there on, extremely interesting and fertile relationships have been developed between physics and mathematics. We have learned to make organizing propositions of the physical world like never before. Someone who, like Newton, is mainly preoccupied with metaphysics, believes that the latter is reality as such; someone more laic would rather say: this is construction of knowledge, with all the objectivity of modern science, but with its own specific conceptual and practical instruments, and so with its own dynamic and evolution. In Einstein's relativity, this causal relationship is profoundly altered and, in a certain sense, it is inversed: it is the acceleration over a geodesic in curve Riemannian varieties which, by producing a field, induces a force. A formal symmetry, the equation, is broken in various ways (reversed in some cases), thus changing intelligibility (and physics). These are great successes of the relationship between physics and mathematics. In reference to the mathematical modelization of physical phenomena, in [3], we further highlight the role of symmetries and their breakings in the analysis of physical causality.

Imitation is something different, and Turing puts it quite nicely: imitation is a construction which does not claim to make the phenomenon intelligible, by proposing a causal structure for it (or better, symmetries or symmetry breakings). Imitation *resembles* causality, it can even be indistinguishable from it, but it does not assume any obligation towards it, towards this aspect of physical intelligibility of what is observed or imitated. For example, if you throw a coin, you will get a sequence of 0s and 1s: you will then be able to *imitate* the process, the sequence, with a random number generator, on a computer. You will have an imitation in the sense where the distribution of probabilities of 0s and 1s is analogous and indistinguishable, for a sequence of reasonable length. One can say that this imitation is excellent, but it has nothing to do with the modelization of a toss of a coin. Because one — the toss of a coin — is the process related to a deterministic system, which is extremely sensitive to the conditions of the environment, to the slightest variation in the parameters at play, and is therefore another paradigmatic example, although a bit different from the previous, of deterministic chaos, and a paradigm of randomness by the extreme sensitivity to border conditions. The other, the computer's pseudo-generator of random numbers, is also a system that is deterministic, but not chaotic: a computer's random number generator is a short one-line program which multiplies sines and cosines, rounds up the results, in a manner inherent to the machine, and produces a sequence of 0s and 1s, *seemingly* distributed at random. But there is nothing random to the process, as opposed to the completely unpredictable toss of a coin: if you click "restart" while leaving all of the machine's parameters identical (something quite possible, even most easy), the supposedly random series will in fact be an identical reproduction, according to the arithmetic law/determination written into the program, which unfolds in the realm of the discrete. The process is Laplacian and is predictable, by iteration, identically, as a time symmetry shift. You will never manage to reproduce such a succession of 0s and 1s with a second launch sequence of the same coin. The causal structures differ profoundly, even if the imitation is excellent.

The essential difference resides in the fact that the basis of digital data is exact; it has, "naturally", the discrete topology, that is, its access proceeds bit by well separated bit. Physical measurement is, conversely, and by physical principle, always an interval that is well represented by continuous mathematics (where discrete topology is not "natural"). In chaotic deterministic systems, a fluctuation/variation below the interval of measurement induces radically different evolutions for the system. This, Turing observes in the 1950s, is theoretically *avoidable* in the Discrete State Machine he has invented and as he named it in those years (and such is also the case in practice: iteration and portability of software, a fundamental form of iteration, work; see [16] for references and further reflections; note that in the 1930s Turing had called his machine the Logical Computing Machine).

3.1. *Models, processes, and unpredictability*

The notion of chaotic dynamics is a mathematical notion and, as we recalled above, it is possible to give a precise definition of a dynamical chaotic system, determined by one or several equations or, more directly, by an evolution function (an endomorphism of a metric or topological space) with the properties enumerated in the note. Unpredictability, on the other hand, is given in the interface between a physical process and mathematics: in order to be able to speak of unpredictability, it is necessary to try to predict (pre-dicere, in Latin), by means of mathematics, the evolution of a phenomenon, a physical one, typically. A process is not unpredictable in itself, without an attempt to account for it or to predict it by means of a mathematical system. On the other hand, a system of functions or a mathematical function is not unpredictable in itself either, as some claim. On the contrary, theorems demonstrate that each Cauchy problem, a very large class of differential equations or, more generally, any reasonable system of equations (or of functions) that is expressible and has a solution, has a computable one. And it is indeed necessary to look attentively to find a system of equations with computable coefficients, of course, having non-computable solutions (see [13] for references). In fact, staying in the field of mathematics, we *compute*, and if we have good theorems of existence (and unicity, if possible) of solutions, we can predict the evolutions, *point* by *point*, each time that computable data is provided to the given system. Mathematics is written in an finite and effective language, even when speaking of infinity: it is very difficult, if we do not make efforts by using stratagems and tricks, to mathematically provide a non-computable function or number (we only know of diagonal tricks, since Turing).

In general, thus, any mathematical determination (by a system of equations, by an evolution function) is computable, hence predictable, when it is given a computable input. And randomness, *within* mathematics, only happens at infinity. In short, an *infinite* sequence is Martin-Löf random when it passes all the *effective* tests (for a recent survey, see [19]): its initial (finite) segments will be just *uncompressible*; they coincide with their shortest formal generation program rather than being random, for the very reason that they are generated by a program (by the finite sequence itself) and are therefore predictable. It is necessary to have an underlying physical process in order for a *finite* sequence or for the production of a single number (the 0s or 1s of a toss of a coin) to be considered as random: unpredictability then, and hence even finite randomness, is once again the result of a friction between mathematics and the world. In a system of equations or for an evolution function, having no reference to a physical process, but which satisfy the mathematical definition of chaotic determination, randomness is *asymptotic*, as is Martin-Löf type of randomness (which is well defined at *infinity*).

The problem is precisely that of the intended meaning of the given mathematical formalism, that is, of the relationship to the process one wants to formalize/modelize. Or, better, in the measurement which enables to pass from the physical process to the mathematical system. When this is an interval, one cannot provide the mathematical model with an exact value, even less than with an integer or with a computable number and, in non-linear dynamics, the input interval is "mixed" and (exponentially) extended through the evolution (over time, generally). This makes the modeling mathematical system obviously computable, but unable to predict the evolution of the modelized physical process. This does not prevent very important *qualitative* information from making formalization of great interest (this is Poincaré's geometry of dynamical systems, but Hadamard as well should be quoted, for his early work on the geodetic flow on hyperbolic surfaces).

To summarize, it does not make sense to speak of the unpredictability of a mathematical system, even a chaotic one, if it is not in relationship with a (presumed) physical process which it modelizes: it is the latter which will be unpredictable (relatively so); the mathematics, for their part, are (almost always) computable. There are also systems and processes which are deterministic and predictable, that is, Laplacian ones: in this category we find processes of which the modelization is well expressed by linear (continuous) systems, or by systems of which the relevant databases are discrete. In both cases, the problem of measurement does not have any important consequence (linearity: the interval is not "mixed") or is not an issue (discreteness: each datum is well separated and accessible, exactly).

In the second case, the difference, I insist, is due to the exact nature of the discrete database, "digit by digit", well separated the ones from the others, without the problem of measurement: its "natural" topology (and the term "natural" has a mathematical sense) is discrete, it isolates each point from the other and enables to access it with exactitude). By physically realizing Turing's *discrete state* machine, we dared to invent a physical process where measure is exact, in contrast to what happens for all (classical) processes.[2] Moreover, iteration, which is also a form of prediction, is a constitutive principle of computer science, daughter of formal arithmetics: Herbrand and Gödel's primitive recursion, since 1930–1931, when the first ideas on computability appear, is iteration (in addition to the updating of a register). The portability of software is also a question of iteration, as we said: one wants to be able to run an expensive program identically, so that it may perform adequately and do always exactly the same thing. On the other hand, we summarize and insist, the physical measure (classical and relativistic) is not an integer, but always an interval, which we represent better by means of a Euclidean

---

[2]Unfortunately, computer scientists, reverse the names and call exact in reference to physical measure (in a continuum), and approximated the round-off.

topology within a continuum: a fluctuation/variation below the interval, therefore an inaccessible one, causes different evolutions in deterministic non-linear or chaotic systems. And in non-linear continuous dynamics, what is most interesting is exactly the role of variation, if possible under the threshold of physical observability, as Turing remarked in his 1952 paper, a pioneer in this as in inventing the discrete artificial processes. Obviously, these two different mathematical structures construct different ideas of the world; both being very effective in terms of their own objectives, but remaining profoundly different, at least as for proposed causal relations and symmetry breakings (the round-off is a symmetry breaking, at each step of the computation and this is very relevant in computer modeling of non-linear dynamics).

One who does not make the difference and who identifies the physical process and its various mathematical representations, a double pendulum or the toss of a coin, say, which we understand as a dynamics in the continuum, with discrete computational imitation, even enhanced with pretty virtual images of a rolling coin, loses the intelligibility of both processes, and will not manage to do better. How can one indeed "do better" and introduce randomness into a discrete state machine? Concurrent networks and systems enable better imitations than pseudo-random generators: a network of discrete state machines, typically the Web, or a system of concurrent processes (which concur with a same process and are not *a priori* synchronized by an absolute and common Newtonian clock), that are distributed in space, are indeed immersed in the space-time which we understand better by means of continuous mathematics. The spatio-temporal shifts, even of relativistic type if the network is distributed over the surface of the earth, and multi-tasking, be it local or global, would present phenomena specific to "continuous dynamics". However, if we simulate with network randomness or concurrency the local randomness due to thermal fluctuation in a double pendulum, we will considerably improve the discrete imitation, but will still continue to produce an imitation: we do not take what we consider to be the local *cause*, inaccessible to measurement, of random variation. But it is already better to import, into discreteness which iterates, the classical or relativist randomness of space-time, which does not iterate.

Let us note, by the way, that Turing, in his 1950 article, says twice that his machine "is Laplacian", because, in such machine, determination implies predictability. "In concrete machines also", he insists. Let us restate it like this: prediction is possible, at least by iteration, even if there are tricks, not inherent to either sequential or concurrent calculus, which can nicely imitate randomness. On the other hand, his 1952 system for morphogenesis is profoundly non-Laplacian and such is its most important property, Turing emphasizes: the dynamics of forms always vary, are deterministic and unpredictable, because are very sensitive to the initial conditions.

I spoke earlier of microphysics, and I would like to mention that it is now possible to enhance a computer with the randomness of quantum mechanics, modifying even more deeply the nature of our digital machines, which are deterministic in the Laplacian sense. Actually, it is possible to improve the computational imitation of classical randomness (dice, the coin) with "intrinsic" forms of randomness thanks to quantum physics. We can purchase a box in Geneva which produces 0s and 1s, according to the up spin and down spin of an electron. In this case, the standard theory says: the probability is intrinsic, because it is the theoretical consequence of the principle of indetermination of quantum physics and of quantum measurement, which is always a value of probability. From the standpoint of the analysis of the 0–1 sequence, the probability distribution is analogous. But the difference is radical with regards to both the classical digital computer and to the toss of a coin (the quantum probabilities are "entangled", see [4]. It is then a question of three different structures of randomness which can at best resemble each other by possible reciprocal imitation, but nothing more.[3]

---

[3]In the computer scientist jargon, a formal process is called "non-deterministic" when it is described by a non-functional relation (a non-deterministic Turing Machine, for example: to one input value, there correspond many outputs). We are then simply away from the classical notion of (mathematical) determination, for which a given evolution function or the solution of the intended system of equations, if any, is supposed to be "single-valued". Then and in contrast to the claim by many, in this case randomness and unpredictability are not at stake: the formalism simply does not describe a deterministic process, whether chaotic or not. It is a non-functional formalism, where an input number does not determine an output number, but an entire set of them. Unpredictability and randomness may be called upon if one happens to associate the non-functional relation to, say, the measure of a quantum process: the result then may be considered a possible (random) value amongst probable ones, thus unpredictable, in the interface between mathematics and physical processes, as usual. We then get into quantum randomness, which we mentioned and which differs from classical randomness as related to deterministic chaotic systems, with their peculiar properties of sensitivity to initial conditions etc. In this and many other cases, the conceptual confusion is often remarkable in unexperienced people and lead to the vision of a "Computing Nature". The point is that Frege and Hilbert have forbidden to relate the foundation of mathematics (as logic or formal systems) to physical space and time, or meaning in them, and computing originated from logic, programmatically far away then from natural sciences. Without their courageous step, of which they were largely aware, we would not have these fantastic artifical machines, but we must now be as well aware of the conceptual gap we created by the peculiarities of the arithmetic tool.

4. Calculus, Physics, and Living Phenomena

I hope that everything we have covered, the dualist and alphabetical nature of these extraordinary machines, the specificity of their causal, Laplacian regime as Turing observed, the difference between computational imitation and physico-mathematical modeling, helps to perceive the immense yet singular role of computer science for the sciences. When we see human beings moving or cells developing in a virtual context, I hope the reason why they seem a bit strange is clear: the dynamics of the images, even their aesthetics, gives an intuition of it at first glance: they actually iterate, and that is what produces this sensation of something... artificial and unaesthetic. Indeed, you know perfectly well that if you press "restart", they will make exactly the same movements (when has anyone seen a group of extras on a movie set or a group of monocellulars who, if we produce them again in their Petri, will take exactly the same trajectories, make exactly the same movements?). The astute creator of virtual realities, if required to, will imitate physical (and animal) variation by means of variegated effects (economical, classical pseudo-randomness generators or using temporal shifts by multi-tasking or concurrency), but often, the designer will not think of it and the "restart" will be somewhat disappointing. It is not a question here of life or of "will" *et similia*: I have recently seen some very nice images of lots of balls bumping into each other but... after having pressed the "restart" button, they took the exact same, identical trajectories. Try to make a real swarm of physical balls circulate and bang each other: you will see a different dynamic each time (the programmer immediately improved the imitation in question, by means of network's randomness). One must be cautious, because what I am trying to describe is an evocative problem, an issue for the imagination, one of great scope: it is a play between the representation, the model, and the imitation of dynamics that is at the center of scientific intelligibility and, I would add, of human intelligibility. Without speaking of human movements which are not balls and which are complicated by a series of other causal elements, as always among living phenomena. This, for intelligibility, is a huge problem that has not yet been fully analyzed. Computational simulations cost a lot less than experiments: hence, many physicists renounce to conducting experiments and work only on implementations. The simulation of turbulence, an extreme case of chaos, not only enables to save on wind tunnels, but its iterability is also an asset: the expert's qualitative judgment at a glance may require as many iterations as necessary in order to appreciate the behavior of an airplane's wing or of the cockpit, and the small variations induced give a good appreciation of the dynamic's sensitivity (but this does not enable to analyze an assemblage of wing and cockpit: virtuality in this case is too far removed from the phenomenon which is excessively complex).

The debate in physics in this regard becomes more profound and with intelligence: theorems of stability or of "shadowing" (the physical or continuous trajectory "follows" the virtual trajectory), in some cases, make explicit that which discrete simulations show us: the analogies and differences with regard to processes which we understand better by means of the analysis of the non-linear continuum.

To summarize, in computational imitation one can have a very original detachment from the world, which is a possible asset if it is well understood. The digital world is an extraordinary invention, as important as the alphabet of which it is a further extension, as I was saying. But we should know how to remain in our knowledge, how to grasp its originality with regard to previous history or the way our knowledge re-proposes each time a different perspective on the world: like the alphabet, which did not exist prior to its very audacious invention, the computer is a very original proposition by mankind, it shapes our way of constructing knowledge, it marks it with its own constitutive logic, its own causal regime. We are now able to construct, by means of imitation, absolutely fantastic structures that are, if completely static, true models. However, it must be clear that, each time a dynamic is involved, the imitation can differ completely from the modelization. What is needed is only some element of a non-linear dynamic or a bit of something human (or animal). In physical (and biological) dynamics, variation also counts, and very much so; in particular, the variation below the threshold of observability, which rapidly modifies the same observable processes. The computer, which has a single "intrinsic" level of observability, that of digital round-off, which is specific to its discrete data structure, does not know how to capture such a variation, the one which counts the most in sensitive dynamics, and for this reason, it can iterate in an always identical manner.

In the imitation of living phenomena, the problem is particularly serious. If we perform a virtual animation of a living organism, we will right away have the impression that something is wrong, as I was saying, because *variability* is at the center of life, exactly in the way that identical iteration is at the center of digital computation. What counts in living phenomena, is that a cell is never identical to a mother cell: the orgin of the phylogenetic drift; then, we have Darwinian selection. At the cognitive level, an action is never identical to a preceding action, though it may sometimes bear a close resemblance. The difference in this case is particularly marked, also with regard to the physical notion of variation, because variability includes the individuation of living entities (its "specificity" with regard to the "genericity" of the physical experimental object, see [3]). Although, there does exist in living phenomena a very rigid chemical fragment of phylogenetic memory, DNA, it is only a component of the ontogenetic dynamic: with RNA and non-linear reciprocal interactions, it is at the origin of the proteinic cascades which occur during mitosis, meiosis, and embryogenesis, in one of the most complex and least understood dynamics there are. DNA is of course a very important component from the hereditary point of view but, from the cell structure to the epigenetic context, many other factors contribute to ontogenesis; particularly, a multitude of irreproducible and irreversible dynamics, which are at the center of the variability of living phenomena. In this case also, the presumed Democritean alphabet and the notion of program are absolutely insufficient (*causally incomplete*, see [17]) for understanding the biological dynamic in which non-reversible and uniterable processes contribute in an essential way to the production of ontogenetic and phylogenetic variability, without which there would be no evolution nor life.

I would like to insist here on a later distinction and precision concerning the more general difficulty of making life intelligible using our current mathematical tools. Mathematics is a science of invariants and of the transformations preserving them. We begin with rotations, translations, Euclidean homotheties that preserve symmetries, up to transformation groups and invariants, as in Klein's classifications of various Riemannian geometries (Euclidean, elliptic, hyperbolic). The (mathematical) theory of categories explains this well, by identifying the objects (invariants) and the transformations which preserve them (morphisms, functors, natural transformations). Discrete mathematics, and hence computer science, adds invariance to this by iteration, a sort of symmetry by temporal translation. What can one say when mathematics, constructed this way, are applied to the analysis of living phenomena? Where can one find as much conceptual and physical stability? At the phenomenal level, life exists precisely by opposite properties: next to "structural stability", a very weak form of invariance, variability is perhaps the main "invariant", because without it there would be no phylogenetic drift, in other words, no evolution. And no ontogenesis, with its variability and non-iteratability of relevant processes. Structural stability does not have the characteristics of mathematical invariance, despite the attempts by René Thom to grasp it using the instruments of Singularity Theory (and the successes in the analysis of the morphogenesis of some organs, in phyllotaxis in particular).

The efforts of some research groups (including mine) consist in identifying the invariants that are specific to living phenomena and are insufficiently described by current physico-mathematical theories. We speak of this in the book we mentioned, where we put the emphasis on the great temporal, even inter-specific invariants, and also on a notion derived from physics, but which is unsuitable for known physical dynamics, that of the "extended critical situation". Living phenomena, we conjecture and try to express rigorously, would find itself in a singular mathematical situation in the technical sense, usually punctual in mathematics, but yet extended, in this case, in a non-zero measure space, a spatio-temporal interval.

5. But... Natural Processes Compute?

Let us take once more a step back into history. In the 1930s, from the works of Herbrand and Gödel, numerous formal systems for computability enabled to make rigorous the intuitions of the founding fathers of mathematical logic (Peano and Hilbert, among others): the deductive certainty of mathematics lies in its potential mechanization. It was then an issue of associating with formal deduction, so clearly defined by Hilbert and his school, an adequate mathematical notion of *effective calculus* or of "potentially mechanizable". And this in the domain of systems based on arithmetics, which Frege and Hilbert had set at the center of the foundational project, and for good reasons at that: the profound crisis which toppled the geometrical certitudes of Euclidean space. Over the course of the following years, Church, Kleene, and others proposed other logico-formal systems, which were apt to grasp this originally informal notion of effective deduction. The breakthrough however, the forerunner of computer science, occurred in the years 1935–1936: at that time, Turing invented his "abstract" machine, and Turing and Kleene demonstrated the equivalence of various formalisms for effective calculus, all being grounded on integer arithmetics, of course. But why would the TM, beyond the demonstrated universality (invariance) of computational systems, have such an important role for the successive developments of computer science? Well, some other formalisms would in fact be much better, from several points of view, and more interesting from the mathematical standpoint.

The lambda calculus by Church, for example, possesses "specific theorems" which are very interesting (Church–Rosser, normalization...) and which rigorously correlate the notion of calculus to that of formal proof, which is the aim of such works (certainty in a proof is the effective computability of it, they said). Conversely, the TM does not possess interesting theorems of its own and if it is used for purposes of demonstration, for complexity analyses for instance, one is eager to prove that they are independent from the chosen computational formalism (modulo some "simple" translations). But Turing's system expresses better than any other the nature of the effective computation: it is a writing-re-writing of the *numbers* and of the very *rules* for the calculation. The logical Computing Machine, as the author calls it in 1936, writes or deletes 0s or 1s, moves a read/write head one notch to the left or to the right over a ribbon, by changing its internal state at each step, on the basis of a finite set of instructions (here is the afore-mentioned distinction between hardware — ribbon and head — and software, the instructions: write, delete, move left-right, change state etc.).

Inspired by Gödel, Turing codifies also the instructions with 0s and 1s: on the ribbon, the instructions themselves can be written and modified, as numbers. A machine whose ribbon has instructions and inputs written on it and which is programmed to apply the former to the latter, the universal machine, will become the model for modern compilers and operating systems, in short, the model for computer science, even current. Hence, its mathematical and practical importance: it makes explicit the computation in its elementary and simple components, as transformation of numbers and of programs on numbers, them too being codified by numbers. And this because the calculation is the *writing–re-writing of numbers.*

Yet, some claim that Nature computes. What sense does it make then to wonder if this table, a waterfall, a strike of lightning, a falling body, a double pendulum, an electric current, a growing tree, a quantum dynamic... any natural process, computes? To make them compute, it is necessary, first of all, to decide where is the input (when the computation begins), where it ends (the output), and then associate numbers to them. In other words, it is necessary to associate these pre-chosen input–output states/instants to numbers by means of physical *measurement.* Since Riemann–Einstein or Poincaré and Planck, it had been understood that this process, the measurement, has a huge importance for physics: reference systems and measure are crucial in relativity; the evolution of a chaotic dynamic can depend on fluctuations or variations below the threshold of possible measurement; quantum indetermination, a key property of measurement, has changed microphysics. But Frege and Hilbert have forbidden us to think to the guys above when doing foundations of mathematics, as if this foundation could be detached from that of physics (see [3]) and lead us to excellent mathematics (logic), to a fantastic digital device and... to the catastrophic philosophy of nature that largely accompanied logic and computing or their vulgarization (the brain, the DNA, the Universe... are a big logical computing machine; a Laplacian one, of course[4]).

I think that, as first approximation, we should, instead, assert that

no natural process computes.

And this is due to the key issue, for modern non-Laplacian physics: the issue of measure and access to phenomena. Yet, following a path that went from the invention of the number, of course rooted in pre-human, animal practices of "small-scale counting", and from the writing of the number and of the alphabet which alone enabled to conceive the numeric codification of meaningless letters,[5] we have achieved the masterpiece of formalizing the alphanumeric Cartesian dualism which is the TM. Then, we were able to transfer such a logico-mathematical invention to physical machines, using artificial processes that are truly original, having the rare quality of evolving by discrete states, a quality obtained with great intelligence by means of valves and transistors, diodes and chips. Therefore, at each moment, the access to the data is exact, measurement is certain (and easy), and does not present the problems of continuous dynamics, as Turing observes with a rare lucidity in his 1950 article (only under the bias and the myths of Artificial Intelligence one could fail to grasp his point, see [16] where that paper is understood in parallel with the 1952 paper by Turing [22]), nor does it present the problems associated with quantum processes. In short, to make non-Laplacian, dynamic or quantum processes "compute", it is necessary to take measurements, and this is a crucial issue for both theories. The huge problem of modern "quantum computing" is precisely that "what is computed is not what is measured". In other words, the evolution of a

---

[4]Fortunately, some have started to reverse the trend and open logic to the world. By symmetries in rules, for examples, or by ideas inspired from the non-commutative geometry, based on quantum non-commutative measurement.

[5]In the many Chinese war treaties there exists no cryptography, already present with Caesar or in the biblical Kabala; at most, in Chinese, a concept would be evoked instead of another, in order to deceive the enemy who remained uninformed of the ambiguity game.

system, described for instance by Schrödinger equations, occurs in Hilbert
spaces with complex values and formal calculations, for example, the sums
that express quantum superposition, are performed within the field of
complex numbers. Measurement, on the other hand, is performed within
the field of real numbers, by taking the modules of complex values and by
losing that which constitutes the very structure of entanglement. This is the
conceptual barrier which still fails to make the numerical use of quantum
superimposition or entanglement phenomena something topical: in other
words, we are still theoretically far from obtaining, after the measurement,
the numeric (real) results which fully use quantum non-separability (the
original contribution of quantum computing).

It is obvious that some physical phenomena, Laplacian or linear ones
for example, enable an easy and effective association of numbers to process
and that it is therefore possible to say that they "compute". In chemistry,
say, the processes of molecular interaction may be exhaustively described
by "discrete state" systems (atom by atom), to a point of making a
great part of theoretical chemistry into a "system of alphabetic rewriting".
Nonetheless, in general, the problem of measurement or the production
of data from the world, a challenge of modern physics, is not an issue
within the inventive audacity of *discrete state*, digital, computer science.
Addressing this problem confers precise meaning to otherwise vague and
wild imaginings about computation and nature: in order to associate a
physical process to numbers and to an input/output computation, it is
necessary to perform a measurement.

And here lies one of the reasons for the lack of success of analogous
computations. Created prior to Turing's type of discrete computability,
the Differential Analyzer by V. Bush from MIT was, for example, and
since 1931, a splendid system of analog integration (a little bit in the way
that a surface "computes" a curve's integral): it was later on developed by
Shannon in 1944 as the general purpose analog computer (GPAC). But,
once again, the approximation of the measurement, the low effectiveness
of the underlying continuous process, the uncertainty of iterability and
portability, all these blocked its developments. And there were probably
other reasons too, such as the effectiveness of digital technology (its
compressibility and its varied codificability: how can one analogically
transfer via a telephone cable the equivalent of 20 megabytes, thus
providing digital TV, the Internet and unlimited phone services?), but also,
maybe, the conveyance of an arithmetico-linguistic prejudice. Mathematical
certainty lies in arithmetics, all foundationalists will say from Frege and

Hilbert onwards; knowledge is in language, will say Frege and the analytical philosophers, especially from the Vienna podium; language, broken down in the alphabet, is codified in arithmetics (Gödel and Turing). And the virtuous-vicious circle sets in, excluding the rest: arithmetics language (arithmetic) machine and back.

To return to the alphabet, to think that natural processes compute is like thinking that we produce sequences of letters when we speak. It is a "comic strip" vision of language; western comic strips, that is, because Chinese children certainly think that when speaking, humans produce ideograms which are concepts and sounds, as in their comics. And we do emit a continuous song, decomposed by our very audacious ancestors from Mesopothamia into a musical-alphabetic notation, who linked writing and song together by means of the phoneme. An undertaking with deep historical roots, yet conventional. Try transcribing an animal's cry or song: in the four languages which come to my mind, the dog's bark is transcribed as bau-bau, arf-arf, bu-bu, woof-woof. However, I have observed that dogs do bark the same way in the four countries in question. The transcription of Keshua, an exclusively spoken Andean language, was a difficult and highly controversial undertaking, for being transcribed into Latin letters (and why not into Arabic or Jewish alphabets? a pure contingency of history). Typically, Spanish phonemes were forced upon it, while modeling, while forcing it into a stream and transforming the language which had an obviously very original musicality. No, we do not produce letters when speaking, in the same way that natural processes do not produce numbers and do not compute, and the *mediation of measurement* is a critical node. Grasping this point is essential to making the most of our extraordinary human logico-mathematical and then physical invention, the discrete state arithmetic machine, the electronic-digital calculator. And maybe, begin to think of the next machine: history is not over, with digital computability.

6. Mnemonic Interlude

After an excess of mathematical evocations, I would like to comfort the reader by brushing, briefly and less formally, the issue of memory. It is a curse that the same word is used in reference to animal (human) memory and to digital databases. The difference is abysmal indeed. What is most important in human (and animal) memory is forgetfulness. Forgetfulness is constitutive of invariance and, therefore, of conceptual abstraction, because in this way, we can forget the details, that which are "unimportant". Let me explain. We do not remember an image, an event, pixel by pixel, exactly. Our view or understanding is *intentional*, from the onset, that is, that there is a "goal", an objective to our comprehension or emotions, an intent in our reading of the world which is always active, and which selects that which must be preserved by memory, that which is of interest. Our perception of the world is always a hermeneutic. Memory, moreover, evokes and causes one to re-live events by reconstructing, each time at least a little bit differently, the image, the event, by interpolating, by revisiting meaning, by emphasizing one trait instead of another. Never will memory reproduce experience exactly, pixel by pixel. And so memory contributes to abstracting "that which counts", it proposes and constitutes invariants, that is, traits, gestures, "Gestalts" and then relatively stable concepts, which language and writing contribute to make common and to later stabilize, to make them relatively independent from transformations in the ecosystem.

And so it re-constructs while forgetting the relatively insignificant elements, those which are insignificant with regard to our goals, by jettisoning that which is useless. This way, we can recognize a school mate 30 years later thanks to his smile, which is a movement, or thanks to a certain tilt of the head, or a fold which forms under his eyes when he speaks. These are dynamics which are all important in our old affective rapports. Pixel by pixel, this face has nothing in common with the one from 30 years earlier: movements, selected by us as invariants and intentionally meaningful, are all that remain. But that is enough for us, and it is precisely what counts: to have forgotten the exact face, in this case, is fundamental in order to recognize the new, because the old one and its details no longer exist. And all this is the opposite of digital memory, which must be exact: what a disaster it would be if, when opening a file a year later, a comma was to be in a different place. What a disaster it would be if a Web page, opened a second time, were to be scrambled due to a memory or communication failure. In computer science, everything is done in order for databases (and communication) to be exact, pixel by pixel. The Web (Internet), this extraordinary "database" for humanity, potentially available to all, must be exact: there lies its strength. Of course, even the Web is dynamic and "forgetful": sites will appear and disappear, and they are modified. But, this will be due to human intervention: the network of machines must have, in itself, an exact and perfect memory. This is the opposite of intentional, selective and constitutive dynamic of meaning and invariance, in the variability, in the active forgetfulness which is animal memory, in which the forgetting of irrelevant details contributes to the construction of the relevant invariant, the very intelligibility of the world. The extraordinary interest of the Web resides precisely in its role as complement (for its originality as a human invention, in my view one as important as the invention of the printing press) to the forgetfulness and the dynamic of our animal memory a memory which language, writing and the printing have already considerably enhanced for mankind, by contributing to its stabilization. What a mistake to believe that the relevance of digital computing was to be the artificial copy or replacement of human intelligence: it did much more, it enriched it in a revolutionary way.

7. Conclusion: A Question of Principles

In this short presentation, we have attempted to highlight some "principles" or foundational elements which govern great mathematical options for the intelligibility of natural phenomena. If we consider the objective of this informal remarks, being mainly computer-science oriented, we have not addressed with sufficient detail the direct and highly fecund relationship between mathematics and physics, even if it was always in the background. Specifically, we have only brushed upon the resemblance of the great principles of conceptual construction, between physics and mathematics, which justify the "very reasonable" effectiveness of mathematics in physics (there are, as to say, "co-constituted", as stressed in [3], in contrast to the arithmetized foundation, Frege-Hilbert style). And only will such an analysis enable to better grasp the limits of mathematical or digital modelization in biology, even to move forward, maybe with new ideas (and conceptual structures). The identification of order or symmetry principles, in mathematics, or the highlighting of the foundational role, in physics, of the geodesic principle, as we did in [3], must be developed in order to grasp "that which underlies" and which unifies or distinguishes whole branches of knowledge, the choice of methods and of instruments, explicit and implicit, the constitution of their meaning or the "origin", in an often more conceptual than historic sense, but also in a historical sense. And this in order to question these very principles, if necessary and if that enables to make other fragments of the world intelligible. Indeed, on the one hand, understanding that common construction principles, from Euclid to Riemann and to Connes (the major name in contemporary geometry of quantum mechanics), on the basis of the access to and measurement of space (from Riemann's rigid body to Heisenberg's non-commutative matricial algebra, to which Connes refers), by founding geometric organization, reinforces the sense of each corresponding theory, all the while grasping the radical changes of perspective provided by each of these approaches. Likewise, the fact of highlighting that the geodesic principle may make intelligible a scientific span going from Copernic and Kepler to Schrödinger's equations (derivable from Hamiltonian optimality, as are Newton's equation, in suitable abstract spaces) enables to grasp, in a single glance, the strength of the theoretical proposition in modern physics, in its successive developments. On the other hand, the "foundational" operation, which counts for us too, consists in a critical "reflection" upon the principles of each science, of "taking a step to the side", of looking at them from a distance, even in order to put them into question, particularly when turning to other scientific fields.

This is what we do when observing, in the book with Bailly, how the phylogenetic (and, in part, ontogenetic) "trajectories" of living matter must no longer be understood as "specific" (geodesics), but rather as "generic" ("possibilities" of evolution), whereas, it is rather the living individual who is "specific". In other words, in physics, the (experimental) object is generic (a body, a photon... can be replaced by any other, in theory and in experiments) and follows specific "trajectories" (critical geodesics), in opposition to biology. It is a duality with physics which enables to appreciate the necessity of a theory specific to living phenomena and which enriches the underlying physical principles — which also participate to the intelligibility of living phenomena. It is the foundational analysis conducted in the book which should enable to highlight the strength and the limitations of the physico-mathematical and computer science framework, its non-absolute character, and the boundaries of its universality. A framework which therefore needs to be completely re-thought outside of its historical fields of construction: the very fruitful relationship between physics and mathematics.

The aim of a foundational analysis today is certainly not that of the founding fathers who rightly sought certitudes during a period of great foundational crises, particularly that of the crumbling of absolute Euclidean time-space, a goal which was highly justifiable 100 years ago and which was already put into question by a few, including the second Wittgenstein (some still existing logician philosophers reveal rather psychotic traits, in their quest for "unshakable certainties"). Today's aim is rather one of practicing an "ethic" of knowledge, in order to move forward: the duty of each researcher of making explicit the great organizing principles of his or her knowledge, of viewing them with a critical eye, in order to do better, especially by turning towards other scientific fields, where they may be insufficient for understanding or may be put into question, even radically, as happened in both relativity and quantum mechanics. This is the sense of the dynamic universality specific to scientific knowledge, which is quite different from any form of absoluteness.

Particularly, it is important to be cautious with regard to these extraordinary images provided by the discrete state machine: they are rich of knowledge, but propose an understanding of the world which is deeply rooted in the principles of alphabetic representation/reduction and even more so on atomism, dualism, and iterability, which are insufficient today for understanding physical processes, and even less so for understanding those specific to living phenomena. Contemporary science, however, with its technical depth and strength, could not exist without the digital simulation and, in general, without the contribution of computer science: for this reason, it is necessary to develop a scientific analysis of what it says, precisely, by putting aside, in the same way that Vaucanson's mechanical puppets were quickly forgotten, the myths of a computational Universe, of digital calculating brains, of genetic "programs" and other projections of latest available technologies upon phenomena, an increasingly ridiculous reading of the world, with its iteration over the centuries.

References

[1] J. Anandan, Causality, symmetries and quantum mechanics, *Found. Phys. Lett.* **15**(5), (October 2002) 415–438.

[2] K. Alligood, T. Sauer and J. Yorke, *Chaos: An Introduction to Dynamical Systems* (Springer, New York, 2000).

[3] F. Bailly and G. Longo, *Mathématiques et sciences de la nature. La singularité physique du vivant* (Hermann, Paris, 2006) (Introduction in English and in French, downloadable, as Longo's papers below).

[4] F. Bailly and G. Longo, Randomness and determination in the interplay between the continuum and the discrete, Special issue: *Mathematical Structures in Computer Science* **17**(2) (2007) 289–307.

[5] J. S. Bell, On the Einstein-Podolsky-Rosen paradox, *Physics* **1**, (1964) 195.

[6] M. Bitbol, *L'aveuglante proximité du rel* (Flammarion, 2000).

[7] M. Bitbol, *Physique et philosophie de l'esprit* (Flammarion, 2000).

[8] D. Bohm, The paradox of Einstein, Rosen and Podolsky, *Quantum Th.* (1951) 611.

[9] D. Bohm, *La plénitude de l'univers* (Le Rocher, Paris, 1987).

[10] M. Cappuccio, Traces of computational mind: from wax tablets to Turing machine *Géométrie et cognition*, ed. Longo, Editions rue d'Ulm (Tome 124, s.5, 2003) 43–60.

[11] R. L. Devaney, *An Introduction to Chaotic Dynamical Systems* (Addison-Wesley, 1989).

[12] C. Herrenschmidt *et al.*, eds. *L'Orient et nous* (Albin-Michel, 1996).

[13] M. Hoyrup, A. Kolcak and G. Longo, Computability and the morphological complexity of some dynamics on continuous domains. Invited survey, *Theoretical Computer Science* **398** (2008) 170–182.

[14] J. Laskar, Large scale chaos in the solar system, *Astron. Astrophys.* **287**, (1994) L9–L12.

[15] J. Lighthill, The recent recognized failure of predictability in Newtonian dynamics, *Proc. R. Soc. Lond. A* **407**, (1986) 35–50.

[16] G. Longo, "Laplace, Turing and the "imitation game" impossible geometry: randomness, determinism and programs in Turing's test. eds. R. Epstein, G. Roberts and G. Beber, *The Turing Test Sourcebook* (Dordrecht, The Netherlands, Kluwer, 2007).

[17] G. Longo and P.-E. Tendero, The differential method and the causal incompleteness of Programming Theory in Molecular Biology, *Foundations of Science* **12** (2007) 337–366. (a longer french version is in "Evolution des concepts fondateurs de la biologie du XXIe siècle", (Miquel ed.) DeBoeck, Paris, 2008).

[18] M. Mugur-Schächter, On a crucial problem in probabilities, and solution, to appear in *Math. Struct. in Computer Science*, (2009).

[19] C. Rojas, Computability and Information in models of Randomness and Chaos, *Math. Struct. in Computer Science* **18** (2008) 291–307.

[20] C. Sini, *Filosofia e scrittura* (Roma-Bari, Laterza, 1994).

[21] A. M. Turing, Computing machines and intelligence, *Mind*, LIX, **236**, (1950) 433–460.

[22] A. M. Turing, The chemical basis of morphogenesis, *Philo. Trans. Royal Soc.* **B237**, (1952) 37–72.

[23] W. H. Zurek, Decoherence and the transition from the quantum to the classical, *Phys. Today*, (October 1991) 36.

Chapter 4

DETERMINISTIC COMPUTATION
WITH RANDOM G-NETWORKS

EROL GELENBE

Imperial College, London SW7 2BT, UK
e.gelenbe@imperial.ac.uk

ZHI-HONG MAO

University of Pittsburgh, Pittsburgh, PA 15260, USA
maozh@engr.pitt.edu

YANDA LI

Tsinghua University, Beijing 100084, P.R. China

The theory of computation generally considers functions that map discrete denumerable structures into structures, while most practical computation is numerical in scope and deals with real numbers. Computing with real numbers is still the bread and butter of the key computer applications such as medical diagnostics, large science, engineering design, sensing and signal processing, business, commerce, the stock market, and so on. While Turing machines and models derived from the logical behavior of computation provide universal models of computation for discrete structures, one can also consider the question of how to characterize universal models of numerical computation. By describing the "G-Network" or "random neural network" and examining its ability to approximate functions, this paper provides an example of a "universal model" of computation for continuous and bounded functions, and also shows how discrete continuous time stochastic systems can offer intriguing models of computation.

1. Introduction

The G-network (GNN) or random neural network (RNN) was introduced in the late 1980s [5,6,12] based on two different paradigms. The first paradigm was motivated by the need to develop a precise mathematical representation of the apparently spiked and random behavior of most neurons in the mammalian brain. Thus, in this respect, the RNN is one possible model of how the brain computes, which in itself is an important scientific question. The second paradigm that has inspired GNN [9, 10, 13, 14, 17, 25, 29, 30, 32] is that of queueing theory, a topic in probability theory which is over 100 years old, and which is widely used in industry to evaluate the performance of manufacturing systems, service systems, communication networks, etc. Within queueing theory GNN have introduced new paradigms including "negative customers" which destroy work (rather than add additional work as normal customers do), and "triggers" which are special control customers which displace work from one queue to another. In the sequel, we will refer to the models covered by the RNN and G-networks as the GNN, a compromise between the term G-networks and the term RNN.

The GNN is a mathematical model which has a countable and unbounded state space, and in this respect it is an infinite state automaton, with "jumps" between states over time. Furthermore, the GNN operates in continuous time, differing from automaton models whose dynamics is described in discrete unit time steps. Thus, the GNN is also quite different from other models of neuronal computation such as the McCulloch-Pitts "sigmoidal" or so-called "connexionist model". With respect to the Hopfield model, or the Boltzman machine models of neuronal computation inspired by spin glass theory of statistical mechanics, the GNN allows for an infinite number of internal states for each neuron contrary to these earlier models which typically only allow binary values for the internal state of neurons. For a review of classical models of neuronal networks the reader is referred to [3].

Although, the GNN is a discrete state-state space model, it is also a probabilistic model in that transitions from state to state over time do not occur in a deterministic manner but are defined via probability distributions. The probabilistic nature of the model is required by *both of the application areas* which have motivated the model. As we had mentioned earlier, spike trains observed in the neuronal networks of the mammalian brain have an apparent random nature; similarly in complex systems such as the Internet, flows of packets occur at apparently random intervals induced by the numerous complex interactions within such systems and by the unpredictable nature of network users. Thus, the probability distribution of the state of the network, rather than the state itself, is the quantity that can be computed. As a result, even though the underlying structure is discrete, the quantity one is computing is a real number and hence the GNN is also a tool for modeling real-valued rather than discrete computation. As we shall see below, it is in a well-defined sense a universal model of computation in that it can be used to approximate a class of useful functions, i.e. those which are continuous and bounded. Note that the approximation capability of neural networks is a well-known question that has been studied by different authors, for instance in [4].

Several applications to practical problems in information engineering [8, 15, 16, 20–23, 35, 36] have used the GNN because of its ability to store or learn patterns efficiently [12] and because of its ability to act as an optimizing network, i.e. a network whose dynamics reduces some well-defined cost function over time.

In this paper, we review the introductory theory of the GNN and consider two of its extensions: the bipolar GNN (BGNN) [7] and the clamped GNN (CGNN) introduced in [26]. The introductory theory will be presented for the general network that admits feedback loops among its cells or neurons. Then, we will show that the feed-forward CGNN and the BGNN with s hidden layers (total of $s + 2$ layers) can be used to uniformly approximate continuous and bounded functions of s variables. This text relies heavily on the presentation in [33]. In [26], we develop a different approach to show that the clamped and bipolar GNN's have the universal approximation property, using a constructive method which exhibits networks constructed from a polynomial approximation of the function to be approximated. However, the construction in [26] does not offer a scheme to restrict the size of the network as a function of the number of variables s. Thus, the approach we discuss here not only offers a universal approximation for a class of significant numerical functions, but also indicates that the size of the network being used, in numbers of neurons or cells, is proportional to the square of the number of variables of the function. In this sense, we are proposing a "small" universal model of computation.

2. The GNN and Its Extensions

Consider a system consisting of n interconnected "neurons" which communicate via "positive" and "negative" signals. The ith neuron's state $i = 1, \ldots, n$ at time t is represented by its "potential" $K_i(t)$, which is a non-negative integer, and the state of the network at time t, is a vector of non-negative integers $K(t) = (K_1(t), \ldots, K_n(t))$. We will denote by k and k_i arbitrary values of the state vector and of the ith neuron's state.

If $K_i(t) > 0$, then neuron i may "fire" in the interval $[t, t + dt]$ with probability $r(i)dt + o(dt)$, or not fire with probability $1 - r(i)dt + o(dt)$, where $r(i) \geq 0$ is a real number which we call the firing rate of neuron i. This firing activity of different cells at time t occurs independently between cells and only depends on the internal state of the neuron itself. If the neuron fires, the following events occur:

- $K_i(t + dt) = K_i(t) - 1$;
- With probability $p^-(i,j)$, $K_j(t + dt) = K_j(t) - 1$ if $K_j(t) > 0$ and $K_j(t + dt) = 0$ if $K_j(t) = 0$ and
- With probability $p^+(i,j)$, $K_j(t + dt) = K_j(t) + 1$,

where for each i, $\sum_{j=1}^n [p^+(i,j) + p^-(i,j)] = 1 - d_i$, and $0 \leq d_i \leq 1$ is interpreted as the probability that the signal or spike that left neuron i when it fired has not been able to reach another neuron, or has been forwarded out of the network. Note that $p^-(i,j)$ is the probability that the spike leaving neuron i "inhibits" neuron j, while $p^+(i,j)$ is the probability that it excites it. It is convenient to define the excitatory and inhibitory *firing rates* of neurons via the quantities $\omega^+(i,j) = r(i)p^+(i,j)$ and $\omega^-(i,j) = r(i)p^-(i,j)$.

In addition to the firing activity of the neurons, spikes may also enter the network from some outside source and this is represented as follows: In the interval $[t, t + dt]$

- With probability $\Lambda_i dt + o(dt)$ an excitatory spike arrives to neuron i from outside the network and $K_i(t + dt) = K_i(t) + 1$, where $\Lambda_i \leq 0$, or
- With probability $\lambda_i dt + o(dt)$ an inhibitory spike arrives to neuron i from outside the network and $K_i(t + dt) = K_i(t) - 1$ if $K_i(t) > 0$, where $\lambda_i \leq 0$, while $K_i(t + dt) = 0$ if $K_i(t) = 0$.

Again, the assumption is that these external arrival streams of spikes to each cell are independent of each other. We see that in all cases, an inhibitory spike that arrives to a neuron that is quiescent (i.e. whose state has the value zero) has no effect.

Based on these assumptions, the state transitions of the network can be derived as a system of Chapman–Kolmogorov (C–K) equations [1] which describe in precise terms the dynamics or state transitions for the probability distribution:

$$p(k,t) = Prob[K(t) = k | K(0) = k^0], \tag{1}$$

where $k = (k_1, \ldots, k_n)$, $k_i \geq 0$, denotes a particular value of the state vector. Here k^0 is some appropriate initial value of the state and is the equivalent of the "initial" state of an automaton. The C–K equation is the counterpart of the state transition function of conventional finite or infinite automata. Let e_i denote an n-vector each of whose elements are zero, except for the ith element which takes the value $+1$.

For the GNN the C–K equation becomes:

$$\frac{dp(k,t)}{dt} = \sum_{i=1,j=1,i \neq j}^{n} [(p(k + e_i + e_j) + p(k + e_i)1[k_j = 0])\omega^-(i,j)$$
$$+ p(k + e_i - e_j)1[k_j > 0]\omega^+(i,j)]$$
$$+ \sum_{i=1}^{n} [p(k + e_i)(r_i d_i + \lambda_i) + p(k)1[k_i = 0]\lambda_i$$
$$+ p(k - e_i)1[k_i > 0]\Lambda_i] \tag{2}$$

for any vector k, with $k_i \geq 0$ for all $i \in \{1, \ldots, n\}$.

2.1. Stationary or steady-state solution

The first result we present concerns the stationary joint probability distribution of network state:

$$p(k) = \lim_{t \to +\infty} p(k,t). \tag{3}$$

Consider the following system of non-linear equations for $i = 1, \ldots, n$:

$$q_i = \frac{\lambda^+(i)}{r(i) + \lambda^-(i)} \tag{4}$$

$$\lambda^+(i) = \Lambda(i) + \sum_{j=1}^{n} q_j \omega^+(j,i),$$

$$\lambda^-(i) = \lambda(i) + \sum_{j=1}^{n} q_j \omega^-(j,i). \tag{5}$$

Theorem 1 (Theorem 1 of [5]). *If all the q_i, which are the solution of the equation (4) exist and satisfy $0 \leq q_i < 1$, then the stationary joint probability of the GNN state is given by:*

$$p(k) = \prod_{i=1}^{n} (1 - q_i) q_i^{k_i}. \tag{6}$$

Intuitively speaking, the $\lambda^+(i)$ and $\lambda^-(i)$ are the *total average arrival rates* of positive and negative signals to each neuron i. Furthermore, the q_i

is the stationary probability that neuron i is excited and therefore that it is able to fire. Note that the q_i whose form is given above, are expressed as the solution of a *non-linear* system of equations. Therefore, the second result that we will recall concerns the *existence* of the solution presented in Theorem 1. The proof of the following result, given in the Appendix of [12], is based on Brower's fixed-point theorem.

Theorem 2. *There always exists a non-negative solution $(\lambda^+(i) \geq 0, \lambda^-(i) \geq 0)$ to the equation (4).*

2.2. The bipolar GNN or BGNN

The GNN model was extended in [7] by introducing the artifact of "positive and negative" neurons. The resulting Bipolar GNN (BGNN) can also be viewed as the coupling of two complementary standard GNN models. In the BGNN, the two types of neurons have opposite roles.

A positive neuron behaves exactly as a neuron in the original GNN. A negative neuron has a completely symmetrical behavior, namely, only negative signals can accumulate at this neuron, and the role of positive signals arriving to a negative neuron is to eliminate negative signals which have accumulated in a negative neuron's potential. A positive signal arriving to a negative neuron i cancels a negative signal (adds +1 to the neuron's negative potential), and has no effect if $k_i = 0$.

This extension is in fact mathematically equivalent to the original GNN described above, with respect to the specific form taken by the stationary solution (Theorems 1 and 2). However, the use of both positive and negative neurons allows the BGNN to become a convenient universal approximator for continuous functions because of the possibility of using both positive and negative valued functions of the input variables. Let P and N denote, respectively, the indices of the positive and negative neurons in the BGNN. In the BGNN, the state of the network is represented by the vector $k(t) = (k_1(t), \ldots, k_n(t))$, so that $k_i(t) \geq 0$ if $i \in P$ and $k_i(t) \leq 0$ if $i \in N$.

In the BGNN, the emission of signals from a positive neuron is the same as in the original GNN. Similarly, a negative neuron may emit negative signals. A signal leaving negative neuron i arrives to neuron j as a negative signal with probability $p^+(i,j)$ and as a positive signal with probability $p^-(i,j)$. Also, a signal departs from the network upon leaving neuron i with probability $d(i)$. Other assumptions and denotations retain as in the original model. If we take into account the distinction between positive and negative neurons, Theorems 1 and 2 can be summarized as follows for the

BGNN. The flow of signals in the network is described by the following equations:

$$\lambda^+(i) = \Lambda(i) + \sum_{j \in P} q_j \omega^+(j, i) + \sum_{j \in N} q_j \omega^-(j, i), \tag{7}$$

$$\lambda^-(i) = \lambda(i) + \sum_{j \in P} q_j \omega^-(j, i) + \sum j \in N q_j \omega^+(j, i), \tag{8}$$

and

$$q_i = \frac{\lambda^+(i)}{r(i) + \lambda^-(i)}, \quad i \in P, \tag{9}$$

$$q_i = \frac{\lambda^-(i)}{r(i) + \lambda^+(i)}, \quad i \in N. \tag{10}$$

Using a direct extension of the results for the conventional GNN, it can be shown that a non-negative solution $\{\lambda^+(i), \lambda^-(i), i = 1, \ldots, n\}$ exists to the above equations. If the $0 \le q_i < 1$, $i = 1, \ldots, n$, then the steady-state joint probability distribution of network state is given by [7]:

$$p(k) = \prod_{i=1}^{n} (1 - q_i) q_i^{|k_i|}, \tag{11}$$

where the quantity q_i is the steady-state probability that node i is "excited". Notice the $|k_i|$ exponent in the expression which is due to the fact that the $k_i's$ can be positive or negative, depending on the polarity of the ith neuron.

3. Approximation of Functions of One Variable by the GNN with a Bounded Number of Layers

Consider a continuous function $f: [0, 1]^s \mapsto R$ of an input vector $X = (x_1, \ldots, x_s)$. Since, an $[0, 1]^s \mapsto R^w$ function can always be separated into a group of w distinct functions $[0, 1]^s \mapsto R$, we will only consider outputs in one dimension. The sequel of this paper is therefore devoted to how a continuous function $f: [0, 1]^s \mapsto R$ can be approximated by neural networks derived from the GNN model. To approximate f, we will construct s-input, 1-output, L-layer feed-forward GNN's. We will use the index (l, i) for the ith neuron at the lth layer. Furthermore, when we need to specify this, we will denote by M_l the number of neurons in the lth layer.

The network under consideration is organized as follows:

- In the first layer, i.e. the input layer, we set $\Lambda(1,i) = x_i$, $\lambda(1,i) = 0$, $r(1,i) = 1$, so that $q_{1,i} = x_i$, for $i = 1, \ldots, s$.
- In the lth layer $(l = 2, \ldots, L)$, $\Lambda(l,i)$, $\lambda(l,i)$, and $r(l,i)$ are adjustable parameters, and $q_{l,i}$ is given by:

$$q_{l,i} = \frac{\Lambda(l,i) + \sum_{1 \leq h < l} \sum_{1 \leq j \leq M_h} q_{h,j} \omega^+((h,j),(l,i))}{\lambda(l,i) + r(l,i) + \sum_{1 \leq h < l} \sum_{1 \leq j \leq M_h} q_{h,j} \omega^-((h,j),(l,i))} \quad (12)$$

where the connection "weights" $\omega^+(\cdot,\cdot)$ and $\omega^-(\cdot,\cdot)$ are also adjustable parameters.

- In the Lth or output layer there is only one neuron. As suggested in [5], we can use the output function:

$$A_{L,1} = \frac{q_{L,1}}{1 - q_{L,1}} \quad (13)$$

whose physical meaning is that it is the average potential of the output neuron as the output of the network. In this manner, we will have $A_{L,1} \in [0, +\infty)$, rather than just $q_{L,1} \in [0,1]$.

3.1. Technical premises

Before we proceed with the developments concerning GNN approximations, we need some technical results. They are similar to some technical results used in [26] concerning continuous and bounded functions $f: [0,1] \mapsto R$ for a scalar variable x. The generalization to $f: [0,1]^s \mapsto R$ is direct and will be examined in Section 4. The proofs are given in the Appendix.

Lemma 1. *For any continuous and bounded* $f: [0,1] \mapsto R$ *and for any* $\epsilon > 0$, *there exists a polynomial:*

$$P(x) = c_0 + c_1 \left(\frac{1}{1+x} \right) + \cdots + c_m \left(\frac{1}{1+x} \right)^m, \quad 0 \leq x \leq 1, \quad (14)$$

such that $\sup_{x \in [0,1]} |f(x) - P(x)| < \epsilon$ *is satisfied.*

The second technical result concerns the relationship between polynomials of the form (14) and the GNN.

Lemma 2. *Consider a term of the form*

$$\frac{1}{(1+x)^v},$$

for $0 \leq x \leq 1$, and any $v = 1, 2, \ldots$. There exists a feed-forward GNN with a single output neuron $(v + 1, 1)$ and input $x \in [0, 1]$ such that

$$q_{v+1,1} = \left(\frac{1}{1+x}\right)^v. \tag{15}$$

The following lemma shows how an arbitrary polynomial of the form (14) with non-negative coefficients can be realized by a feed-forward GNN.

Lemma 3. *Let $P^+(x)$ be a polynomial of the form (14) with the restriction that $c_v \geq 0$, $v = 1, \ldots, m$. Then there exists a feed-forward GNN with a single output neuron (O) such that:*

$$q_O = \frac{P^+(x)}{1 + P^+(x)}, \tag{16}$$

so that the average potential of the output neuron is $A_O = P^+(x)$.

The fourth technical result will be of use in proving the approximating power of the "clamped GNN" discussed below.

Lemma 4. *Consider a term of the form*

$$\frac{x}{(1+x)^v},$$

for $0 \leq x \leq 1$, and any $v = 1, \ldots, m$. There exists a feed-forward GNN with a single output neuron $(v + 1, 1)$ and input $x \in [0, 1]$ such that

$$q_{v+1,1} = \left(\frac{x}{1+x}\right)^v. \tag{17}$$

We state without proof another lemma, very similar to Lemma 3, but which uses terms of both forms of $1/(1 + x)^v$ and $x/(1 + x)^v$ to construct polynomials. Its proof uses Lemmas 3 and 4, and follows exactly the same lines as Lemma 3.

Lemma 5. *Let $P^o(x)$ be a polynomial of the form*

$$P^o(x) = c_0 + \sum_{v=1}^{m} \left[c_v \frac{1}{(1+x)^v} + d_v \frac{x}{(1+x)^v} \right], \quad 0 \le x \le 1, \tag{18}$$

with non-negative coefficients, i.e. $c_v, d_v \ge 0$, $v = 1, \dots, m$. Then there exists a feed-forward GNN with a single output neuron (O) such that:

$$q_O = \frac{P^o(x)}{1 + P^o(x)}, \tag{19}$$

so that the average potential of the output neuron is $A_O = P^o(x)$.

The next lemma is a technical premise of Lemma 7.

Lemma 6. *For any $(\frac{1}{1+x})^i$ $(0 \le x \le 1, i = 1, 2, \dots)$ and for any $\epsilon > 0$, there exists a function*

$$P_1(x) = b_0 + \frac{b_1}{x + a_1} + \frac{b_2}{x + a_2} + \cdots + \frac{b_r}{x + a_r}, \quad 0 \le x \le 1, \tag{20}$$

where $a_k > 0$, $k = 1, \dots, r$, such that $\sup_{x \in [0,1]} |(\frac{1}{1+x})^i - P_1(x)| < \epsilon$ is satisfied.

Proof. We proceed by induction. For $i = 1$, the conclusion obviously holds. Now assume it is true for $i = j$, i.e. for any $\epsilon > 0$, there exists a

$$P^{(j)}(x) = b_0^{(j)} + \frac{b_1^{(j)}}{x + a_1^{(j)}} + \frac{b_2^{(j)}}{x + a_2^{(j)}} + \cdots + \frac{b_m^{(j)}}{x + a_m^{(j)}}, \quad 0 \le x \le 1, \tag{21}$$

where $a_k^{(j)} > 0$, $k = 1, \dots, m$, such that $\sup_{x \in [0,1]} |(\frac{1}{1+x})^j - P^{(j)}(x)| < \epsilon$.
   Then for $i = j + 1$,

$$\left(\frac{1}{1+x} \right)^{j+1} = \left(\frac{1}{1+x} \right)^j \left(\frac{1}{1+x} \right) = b_0^{(j)} \frac{1}{1+x} + \sum_{k=1}^{m} \frac{b_k^{(j)}}{x + a_k^{(j)}} \frac{1}{1+x}. \tag{22}$$

When $a_k^{(j)} \ne 1$,

$$\frac{b_k^{(j)}}{x + a_k^{(j)}} \frac{1}{1+x} = \frac{b_k^{(j)}}{a_k^{(j)} - 1} \left(\frac{1}{1+x} - \frac{1}{x + a_k^{(j)}} \right) \tag{23}$$

which is in the form of Eq. (20). When $a_k^{(j)} = 1$,

$$\left(\frac{1}{1+x}\right)^2 = \lim_{\eta \to 0} \frac{1}{(1-\eta+x)(1+\eta+x)}$$

$$= \lim_{\eta \to 0} \frac{1}{2\eta} \left(\frac{1}{1-\eta+x} - \frac{1}{1+\eta+x}\right) \qquad (24)$$

which can be arbitrarily approximated by a function of the form (20).

Therefore, $(\frac{1}{1+x})^{j+1}$ can also be approximated by a function in the form of Eq. (20). Through mathematical induction, the conclusion holds for any $i = 1, 2, \ldots$. □

The following lemma is the preparation for the construction of a single-hidden-layered BGNN for the approximation of one dimensional continuous function.

Lemma 7. *For any continuous function $f: [0, 1] \mapsto R$ and for any $\epsilon > 0$, there exists a function $P_1(x)$ in the form of (20) such that $\sup_{x \in [0,1]} |f(x) - P_1(x)| < \epsilon$ is satisfied.*

Proof. This is a direct consequence of Lemmas 1 and 6. □

3.2. *BGNN approximation of continuous functions of one variable*

The technical results given above now pave the way for the use of the Bipolar GNN (BGNN) with a bounded number of layers. Specifically in Theorem 4, we show that a BGNN with a single hidden layer can uniformly approximate functions of one variable. The multi-variable case is discussed in Section 4.

Let us first recall a result from [26] concerning the case when the number of layers is *not* bounded.

Theorem 3. *For any continuous function $f: [0, 1] \mapsto R$ and any $\epsilon > 0$, there exists a BGNN with one positive output neuron $(O, +)$, one negative output neuron $(O, -)$, the input variable x, and the output variable $y(x)$ such that:*

$$y(x) = A_{O,+} + A_{O,-}, \qquad (25)$$

$$A_{O,+} = \frac{q_{O,+}}{1 - q_{O,+}}, \qquad (26)$$

$$A_{O,-} = \frac{-q_{O,-}}{1 - q_{O,-}}, \qquad (27)$$

and $\sup_{x \in [0,1]} |f(x) - y(x)| < \epsilon$. We will say that the BGNN's output uniformly approximates $f(x)$.

Proof. The result is a direct application of Lemmas 1 and 3. Apply Lemma 1 to f and express the approximating polynomial as $P(x) = P^+(x) + P^-(x)$, so that the coefficients of $P^+(x)$ are non-negative, while the coefficients of $P^-(x)$ are negative:

$$P^+(x) = \sum_{i=1}^{m} \max\{0, c_i\} \left(\frac{1}{1+x}\right)^i, \tag{28}$$

$$P^-(x) = \sum_{i=1}^{m} \min\{0, c_i\} \left(\frac{1}{1+x}\right)^i. \tag{29}$$

Now simply apply Lemma 3 to obtain the feed-forward GNN with an output neuron $(O, +)$ whose value is:

$$q_{O,+} = \frac{P^+(x)}{1 + P^+(x)}, \tag{30}$$

and the average potential of the output neuron is $A_{O,+} = P^+(x)$. Similarly, using the non-negative polynomial $|P^-(x)|$ construct a feed-forward BGNN which has positive neurons throughout, except for its output neuron, along the ideas of Lemma 4. Its output neuron $(O, -)$ however is a negative neuron, yet all the parameter values are the same as those prescribed in Lemma 4 for the output neuron, as they relate to the polynomial $|P^-(x)|$. Thus the output neuron takes the value:

$$q_{O,-} = \frac{|P^-(x)|}{1 + |P^-(x)|}, \tag{31}$$

and the average potential of the output neuron is: $A_{O,-} = -|P^-(x)|$, completing the proof. □

The next theorem shows the approximation capability of a BGNN with a single hidden layer.

Theorem 4. *For any continuous function* $f: [0,1] \mapsto R$ *and any* $\epsilon > 0$, *there exists a BGNN of three layers (only one hidden layer), one positive output neuron* $(O, +)$, *one negative output neuron* $(O, -)$, *the input variable* x, *and the output variable* $y(x)$ *determined by* (25) *such that* $\sup_{x \in [0,1]} |f(x) - y(x)| < \epsilon$.

Proof. The result is obtained by using Lemma 7. Applying Lemma 7 to f, we express the approximating function as $P_1(x) = P_1^+(x) + P_1^-(x)$ so that the coefficients of $P_1^+(x)$ are non-negative, while the coefficients of $P_1^-(x)$ are negative:

$$P_1^+(x) = \max\{0, b_0\} + \sum_{k=1}^{r} \max\{0, b_k\} \frac{b_k}{x + a_k}, \tag{32}$$

$$P_1^-(x) = \min\{0, b_0\} + \sum_{k=1}^{r} \min\{0, b_k\} \frac{b_k}{x + a_k}. \tag{33}$$

Now construct a BGNN of three layers: one output layer with one positive output neuron $(O, +)$ and one negative output neuron $(O, -)$ in it, one input layer with one input neuron $(1, 1)$ in it, and one hidden layer with r neurons $(2, 1), \ldots, (2, r)$ in it. Now set:

- $\Lambda(1, 1) = x$, $\lambda(1, 1) = 0$, $r(1, 1) = 1$, $d(1, 1) = 0$,
- $\omega^+((1, 1), (2, k)) = 0$, $\omega^-((1, 1), (2, k)) = 1/r$, $r(2, k) = a_k/r$, $\Lambda(2, k) = a_k/r$, $\lambda(2, k) = 0$, for $k = 1, \ldots, r$,
- $p^+((2, k), (O, +)) = p^-((2, k), (O, +)) = (\max\{b_k, 0\}r)/(2a_k^2 C_{MAX})$, $p^+((2, k), (O, -)) = p^-((2, k), (O, -)) = (|\min\{b_k, 0\}|r)/(2a_k^2 C_{MAX})$, for $k = 1, \ldots, r$, where $C_{MAX} = \max\{1, |b_0|, \frac{|b_k|r}{a_k^2}, k = 1, \ldots, r\}$,
- $\Lambda(O, +) = \lambda(O, +) = \max\{b_0, 0\}/(2C_{MAX})$, $r(O, +) = 1/(2C_{MAX})$, $\Lambda(O, -) = \lambda(O, -) = |\min\{b_0, 0\}|/(2C_{MAX})$, $r(O, -) = 1/(2C_{MAX})$.

It is easy to see that $q_{1,1} = x$, and that

$$q_{2,k} = \frac{a_k}{a_k + x}, \quad k = 1, \ldots, r, \tag{34}$$

$$q_{O,+} = \frac{\frac{P^+(x)}{2C_{MAX}}}{\frac{1}{2C_{MAX}} + \frac{P^+(x)}{2C_{MAX}}} = \frac{P^+(x)}{1 + P^+(x)}, \tag{35}$$

$$q_{O,-} = \frac{\frac{|P^-(x)|}{2C_{MAX}}}{\frac{1}{2C_{MAX}} + \frac{|P^-(x)|}{2C_{MAX}}} = \frac{|P^-(x)|}{1 + |P^-(x)|}. \tag{36}$$

Therefore, $A_{O,+} = P^+(x)$, $A_{O,-} = -|P^-(x)|$, and $y(x) = P_1(x)$, completing the proof. $\qquad\square$

3.3. *CGNN approximation of continuous functions of one variable*

We can also demonstrate the approximating power of a normal feed-forward GNN by just adding a "clamping constant" to the average potential of the output neuron. We call this extension the "clamped GNN (CGNN)" since the additive constant c resembles the clamping level in an electronic clamping circuit. Let us first see the corresponding result from our previous work [26].

Theorem 5. *For any continuous function $f\colon [0,1] \mapsto R$ and any $\epsilon > 0$, there exists a GNN with two output neurons $(O,1)$, $(O,2)$, and a constant c, resulting in a function $y(x) = A_{O,1} + A_{O,2} + c$ which approximates f uniformly on $[0,1]$ with error less than ϵ.*

Proof. Use Lemma 1 to construct the approximating polynomial (14), which we write as $P(x) = P^+(x) + P^-(x)$ where $P^+(x)$ only has non-negative coefficients c_v^+, while $P^-(x)$ only has non-positive coefficients c_v^-:

$$c_v^+ = \max\{0, c_v\},$$
$$c_v^- = \min\{0, c_v\}.$$

Notice that

$$-\frac{1}{(1+x)^i} = 1 - \frac{1}{(1+x)^i} - 1 = \sum_{j=1}^{i} \frac{x}{(1+x)^j} - 1,$$

so that

$$P^-(x) = \sum_{v=1}^{m} |c_v^-| \sum_{j=1}^{v} \frac{x}{(1+x)^j} + \sum_{v=1}^{m} c_v^-. \tag{37}$$

Call $c = c_0 + \sum_{v=1}^{m} c_v^-$ and for some $d_v \geq 0$ write:

$$P(x) = c + \sum_{v=1}^{m} \left[c_v^+ \frac{1}{(1+x)^v} + d_v \frac{x}{(1+x)^v} \right]. \tag{38}$$

Let us write $P(x) = c + P^*(x) + P^o(x)$ where both $P^*(x)$ and $P^o(x)$ are polynomials with non-negative coefficients, and

$$P^*(x) = \sum_{v=1}^{m} c_v^+ \frac{1}{(1+x)^v},$$

$$P^o(x) = \sum_{v=1}^{m} d_v \frac{x}{(1+x)^v}.$$

Then by Lemma 5 there are two GNNs whose output neurons $(O, 1)$, $(O, 2)$ take the values:

$$q_{O,1} = \frac{P^+(x)}{1 + P^+(x)},$$
$$q_{O,2} = \frac{P^o(x)}{1 + P^o(x)}.$$

Clearly, we can consider that these two GNNs constitute one network with two output neurons, and we have $y(x) = c + P^*(x) + P^o(x) = P(x)$, completing the proof. $\qquad\qquad\qquad\qquad\qquad\qquad\qquad\qquad\qquad\qquad\Box$

This result can be extended to the CGNN with only one output neuron by applying Lemma 5. However, let us first consider the manner in which a positive "clamping constant" $c > 0$ can be added to the average potential of an output neuron of a GNN using the ordinary structure of the network.

Remark 1 (Adding a positive clamping constant). *Consider a GNN with an output neuron $\hat{q}$ and an input vector x which realizes the function $\hat{q}(x) = P(x)$. Then there is another GNN with output neuron $Q(x)$ which, for real $c > 0$ realizes the function:*

$$Q(x) = \frac{P(x) + c}{1 + P(x) + c} \qquad (39)$$

and hence, whose average potential is $P(x) + c$. More generally, we can exhibit a GNN with output neuron $Q_1(x)$ whose average potential is $bP(x) + c$, for $b > 0, c > 0$.

Proof. The proof is by construction. We first take the output of the neuron of the original network (whose firing rate is denoted $2r$), and feed it into a new neuron with probability 0.5 as an excitatory signal and with probability 0.5 as an inhibitory signal. We set the firing rate of the new neuron to r, and introduce additional exogenous inhibitory and excitatory arrivals to the new neuron, both of rate rc. As a result we have:

$$Q(x) = \frac{rP(x) + rc}{r + rP(x) + rc},$$
$$= \frac{P(x) + c}{1 + P(x) + c}.$$

As a result, the new neuron's average potential is:

$$\frac{Q(x)}{1 - Q(x)} = P(x) + c$$

and we have been thus able to obtain a new neuron with an added positive "clamping constant" c with respect to the average potential $P(x)$ of the original neuron. The extension to a neuron with average potential $bp(x) + c$ is straightforward. Let the additional neurons firing rate be $R > 0$ rather than r and take its exogenous excitatory and inhibitory arrival rates to be Rc. We then obtain:

$$Q(x) = \frac{rP(x) + Rc}{R + rP(x) + Rc},$$
$$= \frac{\frac{r}{R}P(x) + c}{1 + \frac{r}{R}P(x) + c},$$

so that if we call $b = \frac{r}{R}$, this leads to an average potential of $bP(x) + c$.

$\square$

Theorem 6. *For any continuous function $f : [0,1] \mapsto R$ and any $\epsilon > 0$, there exists a GNN with one output neuron (O), and a constant c, resulting in a function $y(x) = A_O + c$ which approximates f uniformly on $[0,1]$ with error less than ϵ.*

Proof. Use Lemma 1 to construct the approximating polynomial of (14), which we write as $P(x) = P^+(x) + P^-(x)$ where $P^+(x)$ only has non-negative coefficients c_v^+, while $P^-(x)$ only has non-positive coefficients c_v^-:

$$c_v^+ = \max\{0, c_v\},$$
$$c_v^- = \min\{0, c_v\}.$$

Notice that

$$-\frac{1}{(1+x)^i} = 1 - \frac{1}{(1+x)^i} - 1 = \sum_{j=1}^{i} \frac{x}{(1+x)^j} - 1,$$

so that

$$P^-(x) = \sum_{v=1}^{m} |c_v^-| \sum_{j=1}^{v} \frac{x}{(1+x)^j} + \sum_{v=1}^{m} c_v^-. \tag{40}$$

Call $c = c_0 + \sum_{v=1}^{m} c_v^-$ and for some $d_v \geq 0$ write:

$$P(x) = c + \sum_{v=1}^{m} \left[c_v^+ \frac{1}{(1+x)^v} + d_v \frac{x}{(1+x)^v} \right]. \tag{41}$$

Let us write $P(x) = c + P^o(x)$, where $P^o(x)$ is a polynomial with non-negative coefficients. Then by Lemma 5 there is a GNN whose output neurons (O) takes the value:

$$q_O = \frac{P^o(x)}{1 + P^o(x)}.$$

This GNN has only one output neuron, and $y(x) = c + P^o(x) = P(x)$, completing the proof. □

The next theorem shows that a CGNN with a single hidden layer is also a universal approximator for continuous functions on $[0, 1]$. We omit the proof, which follows closely the approach used in the proofs of Theorems 4 and 6.

Theorem 7. *For any continuous function* $f: [0, 1] \mapsto R$ *and any* $\epsilon > 0$, *there exists a GNN of three layers (only one hidden layer), one output neuron* (O), *and a constant* c *called the clamping constant, resulting in a function* $y(x) = A_O + c$ *which approximates* f *uniformly on* $[0, 1]$ *with error less than* ϵ.

4. Approximation of Continuous Functions of s Variables

Now that the process for approximating a one-dimensional continuous functions with the BGNN or the CGNN having a single hidden layer is well understood, consider the case of continuous functions of s variables, i.e. $f: [0, 1]^s \mapsto R$. As a starting point, consider the straightforward extension of Lemma 1 to the case of s-inputs such that there is a polynomial:

$$P(x) = \sum_{m_1 \geq 0, \ldots, m_s \geq 0, \sum_{v=1}^{s} m_v = m} c(m_1, \ldots, m_s) \Pi_{v=1}^{s} \frac{1}{(1 + x_v)^{m_v}}, \quad (42)$$

with coefficients $c(m_1, \ldots, m_s)$ which approximates f uniformly. We now extend Lemma 2 to Lemma 8 and Theorem 8 which are given below.

Lemma 8. *Consider a term of the form*

$$\frac{1}{(1 + x_{z1})^{m_{z1}}} \cdots \frac{1}{(1 + x_{zK})^{m_{zK}}}$$

for $0 \leq x_{zj} \leq 1$, *positive integers* $m_{zj} > 0$ *and* $j = 1, \ldots, K$. *There exists a feed-forward GNN with a single output neuron* $(\mu + 1, 1)$ *and input* $x \in [0, 1]$

such that

$$q_{\mu+1,1} = \frac{1}{(1+x_{z1})^{m_{z1}}} \cdots \frac{1}{(1+x_{zK})^{m_{zK}}}. \tag{43}$$

Proof. Without loss of generality, set $m_{z1} \leq m_{z2} \leq \cdots \leq m_{zK}$. The resulting network is a cascade connection of a set of networks. The first network is identical in structure to the one of Lemma 2, and has $m_{z1} + 1$ neurons numbered $(1,1), \ldots, (1, m_{z1} + 1)$. Now set:

- $\Lambda(1,1) = x_{z1}$, $\Lambda(1,2) = 1/m_{z1}$, and $\Lambda(1,j) = 0$ for $j = 3, \ldots, m_{z1} + 1$,
- $\lambda(1,j) = 0$ for all $j = 1, \ldots, m_{z1}+1$, and $d(1,j) = 0$ for $j = 1, \ldots, m_{z1}$,
- $\omega^-((1,1),(1,j)) = 1/m_{z1}$, and $\omega^+((1,1),(1,j)) = 0$ for $j = 2, \ldots, m_{z1} + 1$,
- $r(1,j) = \omega^+((1,j),(1,j+1)) = 1/m_{z1}$ for $j = 2, \ldots, m_{z1} + 1$,
- Finally, the connection from the first network into the second network is made via $p^+((1, m_{z1}+1),(2,2)) = m_{z1}/m_{z2} \leq 1$, with $d(1, m_{z1}+1) = (1 - m_{z1}/m_{z2})$.

It is easy to see that $q_{1,1} = x_{z1}$, and that

$$q_{1,m_{z1}+1} = \frac{1}{(1+x_{z1})^{m_{z1}}}. \tag{44}$$

The second network has $m_{z2} + 1$ neurons numbered $(2,1), \ldots, (2, m_{z2} + 1)$. Now set:

- $\Lambda(2,1) = x_{z2}$ and $\Lambda(1,j) = 0$ for $j = 2, \ldots, m_{z2} + 1$,
- $\lambda(2,j) = 0$ for all $j = 1, \ldots, m_{z2}+1$, and $d(2,j) = 0$ for $j = 1, \ldots, m_{z2}$,
- $\omega^-((2,1),(2,j)) = 1/m_{z2}$, and $\omega^+((2,1),(2,j)) = 0$ for $j = 2, \ldots, m_{z2} + 1$,
- $r(2,j) = \omega^+((2,j),(2,j+1)) = 1/m_{z2}$ for $j = 2, \ldots, m_{z2} + 1$,
- The connection from the second network into the third network is made via $p^+((2, m_{z2} + 1),(3,2)) = m_{z2}/m_{z3} \leq 1$, with $d(2, m_{z2} + 1) = (1 - m_{z2}/m_{z3})$.

It is easy to see that $q_{2,1} = x_{z2}$, and that

$$q_{2,m_{z2}+1} = \frac{1}{(1+x_{z1})^{m_{z1}}} \frac{1}{(1+x_{z2})^{m_{z2}}}. \tag{45}$$

The remaining construction just pursues the same scheme. $\qquad\square$

Theorem 8. *For any continuous function $f:[0,1]^s \mapsto R$ and any $\epsilon > 0$, there exists a BGNN with one positive output neuron $(O, +)$, one negative* *output neuron* $(O, -)$, *s input variables* $X = (x_1, \ldots, x_s)$, *and the output variable* $y(X)$ *such that*:

$$y(X) = A_{O,+} + A_{O,-}, \tag{46}$$

$$A_{O,+} = \frac{q_{O,+}}{1 - q_{O,+}}, \tag{47}$$

$$A_{O,-} = \frac{-q_{O,-}}{1 - q_{O,-}}, \tag{48}$$

and $\sup_{x \in [0,1]} |f(X) - y(X)| < \epsilon$. *We will say that the BGNN's output uniformly approximates* $f(X)$.

Proof. The proof follows the proof of Theorem 3, using the polynomial of (42). Lemma 7 establishes that the terms of such a polynomial can be realized by a GNN. We then construct two polynomials, one with non-negative coefficients only, and the other with negative coefficients, and show how they are realized with the BGNN. We will not go through the steps of the proof, since it is a step by step duplicate of the proof of Theorem 3. □

We now extend Lemma 7 to the case of s-inputs.

Lemma 9. *For any continuous function* $f : [0, 1]^s \mapsto R$ *and for any* $\epsilon > 0$, *there exists a function of the form*

$$P_s(x) = \sum_{i=1}^{r} \sum_{0 \leq m_1 \leq 1, \ldots, 0 \leq m_s \leq 1} b(m_1, \ldots, m_s, i) \prod_{v=1}^{s} \frac{1}{(a_{v,i} + x_v)^{m_v}}, \tag{49}$$

where $a_{v,i} > 0$, $v = 1, \ldots, s$, $i = 1, 2, \ldots$, *such that* $\sup_{x \in [0,1]} |f(x) - P_s(x)| < \epsilon$ *is satisfied.*

Proof. This is simply an extension of Lemma 7. □

As a consequence we can now establish the following general result.

Theorem 9. *For any continuous function* $f : [0, 1]^s \mapsto R$ *and any* $\epsilon > 0$, *there exists a BGNN of no more than* $s + 2$ *layers* (s *hidden layers*), *one positive output neuron* $(O, +)$, *one negative output neuron* $(O, -)$, s *input variables* $X = (x_1, \ldots, x_s)$, *and the output variable* $y(X)$ *determined by* (46) *such that* $\sup_{x \in [0,1]} |f(X) - y(X)| < \epsilon$.

Proof. The proof is by construction. By Lemma 9, we only need to find an appropriate BGNN of the form as described in Theorem 9 to realize any function of the form (49). We construct a BGNN with s input neurons $(1,1),\ldots,(1,s)$, one positive output neuron $(O,+)$, one negative output neuron $(O,-)$, and M parallel sub-networks between the input layer and the output layer, where

$$M \equiv \sum_{i=1}^{r} \sum_{0 \le m_1 \le 1,\ldots,0 \le m_s \le 1} 1(b(m_1,\ldots,m_s,i) \ne 0), \qquad (50)$$

$1(X) = 1$ when X is true otherwise $1(X) = 0$. Each sub-network is a cascade connection of no more than s neurons. The output of the last neuron of each sub-network takes the value in proportion to each term in function (49).

Without loss of generality, we consider a term of the form

$$\frac{1}{a_{z1} + x_{z1}} \cdots \frac{1}{a_{zK} + x_{zK}} \qquad (51)$$

where $a_{z1} \ge a_{z2} \ge \cdots \ge a_{zK}$. Now, we want to construct a sub-network which has K neurons and of which the last neuron's output takes the value in proportion to the term. Number the K neurons as $(2,1),(3,1),\ldots,(K+1,1)$, and set:

- $\Lambda(1,i) = x_i$, $\lambda(1,i) = 0$, $r(1,i) = 1$, for $i = 1,\ldots,s$,
- $\omega^+((1,z1),(2,1)) = 0$, $\omega^-((1,z1),(2,1)) = 1/M$,
- $r(2,1) = a_{z1}/M$, $\Lambda(2,1) = a_{z1}/M$, $\lambda(2,1) = 0$.

It is easy to see that

$$q_{2,1} = \frac{a_{z1}}{a_{z1} + x_{z1}}. \qquad (52)$$

Then set:

- $p^+((k,1),(k+1,1)) = a_{zK}/a_{z(K-1)}$, for $k = 2,\ldots,K$,
- $\omega^+((1,zk),(k+1,1)) = 0$, $\omega^-((1,zk),(k+1,1)) = 1/M$, for $k = 2,\ldots,K$,
- $r(k+1,1) = a_{zk}/M$, $\Lambda(k+1,1) = 0$, $\lambda(k+1,1) = 0$, for $k = 2,\ldots,K$.

We will find

$$q_{3,1} = \frac{a_{z1} a_{z2}}{(a_{z1} + x_{z1})(a_{z2} + x_{z2})}, \qquad (53)$$

$$\cdots,$$

$$\frac{a_{z1} \cdots a_{zK}}{(a_{z1} + x_{z1}) \cdots (a_{zK} + x_{zK})} \qquad (54)$$

which is in proportion to (51).

Next we connect all the last neurons of the sub-networks to $(O, +)$ or $(O, -)$. The parameter setting follows the steps in the proof of Theorem 4 which connects the neurons in the hidden layer to the output neurons. Since the sub-networks are parallel and each sub-network contains no more than s neurons, there are totally no more than s hidden layers in this constructed BGNN. Thus, we complete the construction. □

We can now obtain Theorems 10 and 11, which generalize Theorems 6 and 7, in a similar manner.

Theorem 10. *For any continuous function* $f : [0, 1]^s \mapsto R$ *and any* $\epsilon > 0$, *there exists a GNN with one output neuron* (O), *and a constant c called the clamping constant, resulting in a function* $y(X) = A_O + c$ *which approximates f uniformly on* $[0, 1]^s$ *with error less than* ϵ.

Theorem 11. *For any continuous function* $f : [0, 1]^s \mapsto R$ *and any* $\epsilon > 0$, *there exists a GNN of no more than* $s + 2$ *layers* (s *hidden layers*), *one output neuron* (O), *and a constant c called the clamping constant, resulting in a function* $y(X) = A_O + c$ *which approximates f uniformly on* $[0, 1]^s$ *with error less than* ϵ.

5. Conclusions

An important requirement for a computational model is that it should offer the ability to compute exactly or approximately, some sufficiently general and useful class of functions. In this paper, we discuss the GNN model and show that it is tool for approximating continuous and bounded real-valued functions.

However, our results are even stronger in the following sense. First, we show that this approximation can be achieved by the feed-forward GNN, i.e. by a network in which only a finite number of past values of the input variables need to be stored. Secondly, and quite intriguingly, we show that the amount of memory needed in the network is actually bounded by the number of input variables of the function.

References

[1] W. E. Feller, *An Introduction to Probability Theory and Its Applications*, Vol. I (3rd Edition) and Vol. II (Wiley, 1968, 1966).

[2]   M. J. D. Powell, *Approximation Theory and Methods* (Cambridge University Press, 1981).

[3]   J. L. McClelland, D. E. Rumelhart, *et al.*, *Parallel Distributed Processing*, Vols. I and II (MIT Press, 1986).

[4]   K. Funahashi, On the approximate realization of continuous mapping by neural network, *Neural Networks* **2** (1989) 183–192.

[5]   E. Gelenbe, Random neural networks with negative and positive signals and product form solution, *Neural Comput.* **1**(4) (1989) 502–511.

[6]   E. Gelenbe, Stability of the random neural network model, *Neural Comput.* **2**(2) (1990) 239–247.

[7]   E. Gelenbe, A. Stafylopatis and A. Likas, Associative memory operation of the random network model, in *Proceedings International Conference Artificial Neural Networks*, Helsinki, 1991, pp. 307–312.

[8]   E. Gelenbe and F. Batty, Minimum cost graph covering with the random neural network, *Comput. Sci. Oper. Res.*, ed. O. Balci (New York, Pergamon, 1992), 139–147.

[9]   E. Gelenbe, Queueing networks with negative and positive customers, *J. Appl. Probab.* **28** (1991) 656–663.

[10] E. Gelenbe and M. Schassberger, Stability of product form G-networks, *Probab. Eng. Inform. Sci.* **6** (1992) 271–276.

[11] V. Atalay, E. Gelenbe and N. Yalabik, The random neural network model for texture generation, *Int. J. Pattern Recogn.* **6**(1) (1992) 131–141.

[12] E. Gelenbe, Learning in the recurrent random network, *Neural Comput.* **5** (1993) 154–164.

[13] E. Gelenbe, G-networks with instantaneous customer movement, *J. Appl. Probab.* **30**(3) (1993) 742–748.

[14] E. Gelenbe, G-networks with signals and batch removal, *Probab. Eng. Inform. Sci.* **7** (1993) 335–342.

[15] E. Gelenbe, V. Koubi and F. Pekergin, Dynamical random neural network approach to the traveling salesman problem, in *Proceedings of the IEEE Symposium System, Man, Cybern. 1993*, pp. 630–635.

[16] A. Ghanwani, A qualitative comparison of neural network models applied to the vertex covering problem, *Elektrik* **2**(1) (1994) 11–18.

[17] J. M. Fourneau, E. Gelenbe and R. Suros, G-networks with multiple classes of positive and negative customers, *Theor. Comput. Sci.* **155** (1996) 141–156.

[18] E. Gelenbe, C. Cramer, M. Sungur and P. Gelenbe, Traffic and video quality in adaptive neural compression, *Multimedia Syst.* **4** (1996) 357–369.

[19] E. Gelenbe, T. Feng and K. R. R. Krishnan, Neural network methods for volumetric magnetic resonance imaging of the human brain, in *Proceedings of the IEEE* **84**(10) (October 1996) 1488–1496.

[20] E. Gelenbe, C. Cramer, M. Sungur and P. Gelenbe, Traffic and video quality in adaptive neural compression, *Multimedia Syst.* **4** (1996) 357–369.

[21] C. Cramer, E. Gelenbe and H. Bakircioglu, Low bit rate video compression with neural networks and temporal subsampling, in *Proceedings of the IEEE* **84**(10) (October 1996) 1529–1543.

[22] E. Gelenbe, T. Feng and K. R. R. Krishnan, Neural network methods for volumetric magnetic resonance imaging of the human brain, in *Proceedings of the IEEE* **84**(10) (October 1996) 1488–1496.

[23] E. Gelenbe, A. Ghanwani and V. Srinivasan, Improved neural heuristics for multicast routing, *IEEE J. Sel. Areas Commun.* **15**(2) (1997) 147–155.

[24] H. Bakircioglu, E. Gelenbe and T. Koçak, Image processing with the random neural network model, *Elektrik* **5**(1) (1998) 65–77.

[25] E. Gelenbe and A. Labed, G-networks with multiple classes of signals and positive customers, *Euro. J. Oper. Res.* **108**(2) (July 1998) 293–305.

[26] E. Gelenbe, Z. H. Mao and Y. D. Li, Function approximation with spiked random networks, *IEEE Trans. Neural Networks* **10**(1) (January 1999) 3–9.

[27] E. Gelenbe and J. M. Fourneau, Random neural networks with multiple classes of signals, *Neural Comput.* **11** (1999) 721–731.

[28] E. Gelenbe and T. Koçak, Area-based results for mine detection, *IEEE Trans. Geosci. Remote Sens.* **38**(1) (January 2000) 1–14.

[29] E. Gelenbe, The first decade of G-networks, *Euro. J. Oper. Res.* **126** (October 2000) 231–232.

[30] E. Gelenbe and J. M. Fourneau, G-networks with resets, *Performance Evaluation* **49** (2002) 179–192. Also in *Proceedings of the IFIP WG 7.3/ACM-SIGMETRICS Performance '02 Conference*, Rome, Italy.

[31] E. Gelenbe and K. Hussain, Learning in the multiple class random neural network, *IEEE Trans. Neural Networks* **13**(6) (2002) 1257–1267.

[32] J.-M. Fourneau and E. Gelenbe, Flow equivalence and stochastic equivalence in G-networks, *Comput. Manag. Sci.* **1**(2) (2004) 179–192.

[33] E. Gelenbe, Z.-H. Mao and Yan-Da Li, Function approximation by random neural networks with a bounded number of layers, *J. Diff. Eqs. Dyn. Sys.* **12**(1&2) (2004) 143–170.

[34] H. Abdelbaki, E. Gelenbe and T. Kocak, Neural algorithms and energy measures for EMI based mine detection, *J. Diff. Eqs. Dyn. Sys.* **13**(1&2) (2005) 63–86.

[35] E. Gelenbe, R. Lent and Z. Xu, Design and performance of cognitive packet networks, *Perform. Evaluation* **46** (2001) 155–176.

[36] E. Gelenbe, R. Lent and Z. Xu, Measurement and performance of a cognitive packet network, *Comput. Netw.* **37** (2001) 691–791.

Appendix: Proof of Technical Lemmas

Proof of Lemma 1. This is a direct consequence of Weierstrass' Theorem (see [2], p. 61) which states that for any continuous function $h: [a, b] \mapsto R$, and some $\epsilon > 0$, there exists a polynomial $P(u)$ such that $\sup_{u \in [a,b]} |h(u) - P(u)| < \epsilon$. Now let $u = 1/(1+x)$, $u \in [1/2, 1]$ and select $x = (1-u)/u$ with $h(u) = f(\frac{1-u}{u}) = f(x)$. If $f(x)$ is continuous, then so is $h(u)$ so that there exists an algebraic polynomial of the form:

$$P(u) = c_0 + c_1 u + \cdots + c_m u^m, \quad 1/2 \le u \le 1, \tag{55}$$

such that $\sup_{u \in [1/2,1]} |h(u) - P(u)| < \epsilon$. Therefore $P(x)$ is given by (14), and $\sup_{x \in [0,1]} |f(x) - P(x)| < \epsilon$. $\qquad \square$

Proof of Lemma 2. Construct a feed-forward GNN with $v + 1$ neurons numbered $(1, 1), \ldots, (v + 1, 1)$. Now set:

- $\Lambda(1, 1) = x$, $\Lambda(2, 1) = 1/v$, and $\Lambda(j, 1) = 0$ for $j = 3, \ldots, v + 1$,
- $\lambda(j, 1) = 0$ for all $j = 1, \ldots, v + 1$, and $d(j, 1) = 0$ for $j = 1, \ldots, v$,
- $\omega^-((1, 1), (j, 1)) = 1/v$, and $\omega^+((1, 1), (j, 1)) = 0$ for $j = 2, \ldots, v + 1$,
- $r(j, 1) = \omega^+((j, 1), (j + 1, 1)) = 1/v$ for $j = 2, \ldots, v$,
- Finally, $d(v + 1, 1) = 1$.

It is easy to see that $q_{1,1} = x$, and that

$$q_{j+1,1} = \left(\frac{1}{1+x} \right)^j, \tag{56}$$

for $j = 1, \ldots, v$ so the lemma follows. $\qquad \square$

The next result exhibits a simple construction process for algebraic expressions using the feed-forward GNN.

Remark. *If there exists a feed-forward GNN with a single output neuron* $(L, 1)$, *and a function* $g: [0, 1] \mapsto [0, 1]$ *such that:*

$$q_{L,1} = g(x), \tag{57}$$

then there exists an $L + 1$ *layer feed-forward GNN with a single output neuron* (Q) *such that:*

$$q_O = \frac{g(x)}{1 + g(x)}. \tag{58}$$

Proof. The simple proof is by construction. We simply add an additional neuron (Q) the original GNN, and leave all connections in the original GNN unchanged except for the output connections of the neuron $(L, 1)$. Let the firing rate of neuron $(l, 1)$ be $r(L, 1)$. Then:

- $(L, 1)$ will now be connected to the new neuron $(L + 1, 1)$ by $\omega^+((L, 1), Q) = r(L, 1)/2$, $\omega^-((L, 1), Q) = r(L, 1)/2$,
- $r(Q) = r(L, 1)/2$.

This completes the proof. $\qquad \square$

Proof of Lemma 3. The proof is by construction. Let C_{MAX} be the largest of the coefficients in $P^+(x)$ and write $P^*(x) = P^+(x)/C_{MAX}$. Let

$c_j^* = c_j/C_{MAX} \leq 1$ so that now each term $c_j^* \frac{1}{(1+x)^j}$ in $P^*(x)$ is no greater than 1, $j = 1, \ldots, m$. We now take m networks of the form of Lemma 2 with $r(j, 1) = 1$, $j = 1, \ldots, m$ and output values

$$q_{j,1} = \left(\frac{1}{1+x}\right)^j, \tag{59}$$

and connect them to the new output neuron (O) by setting the probabilities $p^+((j, 1), O) = c_j^*/2$, $p^-((j, 1), O) = c_j^*/2$. Furthermore, we set an external positive and negative signal arrival rate $\Lambda(O) = \lambda(O) = c_0^*/2$ and $r(O) = 1/(2C_{MAX})$ for the output neuron. We now have:

$$q_O = \frac{\frac{P^*(x)}{2}}{\frac{1}{2C_{MAX}} + \frac{P^*(x)}{2}}. \tag{60}$$

We now multiply the numerator and the denominator on the right-hand side of the above expression by $2C_{MAX}$ to obtain

$$q_O = \frac{P^+(x)}{1 + P^+(x)} \tag{61}$$

so that which completes the proof of the lemma. $\square$

Proof of Lemma 4. The proof is very similar to that of Lemma 2. Construct a feed-forward GNN with $v+1$ neurons numbered $(1, 1), \ldots, (v+1, 1)$. Now set:

- $\Lambda(1, 1) = x$, and $\Lambda(j, 1) = 0$ for $j = 2, \ldots, v+1$,
- $\lambda(j, 1) = 0$ for all $j = 1, \ldots, v+1$, and $d(j, 1) = 0$ for $j = 1, \ldots, v$,
- $\omega^+((1, 1), (2, 1)) = 1/(v+1)$, $\omega^-((1, 1), (j, 1)) = 1/(v+1)$ for $j = 2, \ldots, v+1$, and $\omega^+((1, 1), (j, 1)) = 0$ for $j = 3, \ldots, v+1$,
- $r(j, 1) = \omega^+((j, 1), (j+1, 1)) = 1/(v+1)$ for $j = 2, \ldots, v$,
- Finally, $d(v+1, 1) = 1$.

It is easy to see that $q_{1,1} = x$, and that

$$q_{j+1,1} = \frac{x}{(1+x)^j}, \tag{62}$$

for $j = 1, \ldots, v$ so the lemma follows. $\square$

Finally, we state without proof another lemma, very similar to Lemma 4, but which uses terms of the form $x/(1+x)^v$ to construct polynomials. Its proof uses Lemma 5, and follows exactly the same lines as Lemma 4.

Lemma 6. *Let* $P^o(x)$ *be a polynomial of the form*

$$P^o(x) = c_0 + c_1 \frac{x}{1+x} + \cdots + c_m \frac{x}{(1+x)^m}, \quad 0 \le x \le 1, \qquad (63)$$

with non-negative coefficients, i.e. $c_v \ge 0$, $i = 1, \ldots, m$. *Then there exists a feed-forward GNN with a single output neuron* $(O, +)$ *such that:*

$$q_O = \frac{P^o(x)}{1 + P^o(x)}, \qquad (64)$$

so that the average potential of the output neuron is $A_O = P^o(x)$.

Chapter 5

ASSERTIONS: A PERSONAL PERSPECTIVE

TONY HOARE

Senior Researcher, Microsoft Research Ltd.
Cambridge, England
thoare@microsoft.com

An assertion is a Boolean formula written in the text of a program, at a place where its evaluation will always be true — or at least, that is the intention of the programmer. In the absence of jumps, it specifies the internal interface between the part of the program that comes before it and the part that comes after. The interface between a procedure declaration and its call is defined by assertions known as pre-conditions and post-conditions. If the assertions are strong enough, they express everything that the programmers on either side of the interface need to know about the program on the other side, even before the code is written. Indeed, such strong assertions can serve as the basis of a formal proof of the correctness of a complete program.

In this paper, I will describe how my early experience in industry triggered my interest in assertions and their role in program proofs; and how my subsequent research at university extended the idea into a methodology for the specification and design of programs. Now that I have returned to work in industry, I have had the opportunity to investigate the current role of assertions in industrial program development. My personal perspective illustrates the complementary roles of pure research, aimed at academic ideals of excellence, and the unexpected ways in which the results of such research contribute to the gradual improvement of engineering practice.

1. Experience in Industry, 1960–1968

My first job was as a programmer for a small British computer manufacturer, Elliott Brothers of London at Borehamwood. My task was to

---

This chapter is based on "Assertions: A Personal Perspective" by C.A.R. Hoare which appeared in the IEEE Annals of the History of Computing, Vol. 25(2): 14–25, © [2003] IEEE.

write library programs in decimal machine code [1] for the company's new 803 computer. After a preliminary exercise which gave my boss confidence in my skill, I was entrusted with the task of implementing a new sorting method recently invented and published by Shell [2]. I really enjoyed optimizing the inner loops of my program to take advantage of the most ingenious instructions of the machine code. I also enjoyed documenting the code according to the standards laid down for programs to be delivered to customers as part of our library. Even testing the program was fun; tracing the errors was like solving mathematical puzzles. How wonderful that programmers get paid for this too! In fairness, surely the programmers should pay the cost for removal of their own mistakes.

But not such fun was the kind of error that caused my test programs to run wild (crash); quite often, they even over-wrote the data needed to diagnose the cause of the error. Was the crash due perhaps to a jump into the data space, or to an instruction over-written by a number? The only way to find out was to add extra output instructions to the program, tracing its behaviour up to the moment of the crash. But the sheer volume of the output only added to the confusion. Remember, in those days the lucky programmer was one who had access to the computer just once a day. Even 40 years later, the problem of crashing programs is not altogether solved.

When I had been in my job for six months, an even more important task was given to me, that of designing a new high-level programming language for the projected new and faster members of the Company's range of computers. By great good fortune, there came into my hands a copy of Peter Naur's Report on the Algorithmic Language ALGOL 60 [3], which had recently been designed by an international committee of experts; we decided to implement a subset of that language, which I selected with the goal of efficient implementation on the Elliott computers. In the end, I thought of an efficient way of implementing nearly the whole language.

An outstanding merit of Peter Naur's Report was that it was only 21 pages long. Yet, it gave enough accurate information for an implementer to compile the language without any communication with the language designers. Furthermore, a user could program in the language without any communication either with the implementers or with the designers. Even so, it was possible for the program to work on the very first time it was submitted to the newly implemented compiler. Apart from a small error in the character codes, this is what actually happened one day at an exhibition of an Elliott 803 computer in Eastern Europe. Few languages designed since then have matched such an achievement.

Part of the credit for this success was the very compact yet precise notation for defining the grammar or syntax of the language, the class of texts that are worthy of consideration as meaningful programs. This notation was due originally to the great linguist, psychologist and philosopher Noam Chomsky [4]. It was first applied to programming languages by John Backus [5], in a famous article on the Syntax and the Semantics of the proposed International Algorithmic Language of the Zurich ACM-GAMM Conference, Paris, 1959. After dealing with the syntax, Backus looked forward to a continuation article on the semantics. It never appeared: in fact it laid down a challenge of finding a precise and elegant formal definition of the meaning of programs, which inspires good research in computer science right up to the present day.

The syntactic definition of the language served as a pattern for the structure of the whole of our ALGOL compiler, which used a method now known as recursive descent. As a result, it was logically impossible (almost) for any error in the syntax of a submitted program to escape detection by the compiler. If a successfully compiled program went wrong, the programmer had complete confidence that this was not the result of a misprint that made the program meaningless. Chomsky's syntactic definition method was soon more widely applied to earlier and to later programming languages, with results that were rarely as attractive as for ALGOL 60. I thought that this failure reflected the intrinsic irregularity and ugliness of the syntax of these other languages. One purpose of a good formal definition method is to guide the designer to improve the quality of the language it is used to define.

In designing the machine code to be output by the Elliott ALGOL compiler [6], I took it as an over-riding principle that no program compiled from the high-level language could ever run wild. Our customers had to accept a significant performance penalty, because every subscripted array access had to be checked at run time against both upper and lower array bounds; they knew how often such a check fails in a production run, and they told me later that they did not want even the option to remove the check. As a result, programs written in ALGOL would never run wild, and debugging was relatively simple, because the effect of every program could be inferred from the source text of the program itself, without knowing anything about the compiler or about the machine on which it was running. If only we had a formal semantics to complement the formal syntax of the language, perhaps the compiler would be able to help in detecting and averting other kinds of programming error as well.

Interest in semantics was widespread. In 1964, a conference took place in Vienna on Formal Language Description Languages for Computer Programming [7]. It was attended by 51 scientists from 12 nations. One of the papers was entitled "The definition of programming languages by their compilers" [8], by Jan Garwick, pioneer of computing science in Norway. The title appalled me, because it suggested that the meaning of any program is determined by selecting a standard implementation of that language on a particular machine. So, if you wanted to know the meaning of a Fortran program, for example, you would run it on an IBM 709, and see what happened. Such a proposal seemed to me grossly unfair to all computer manufacturers other than IBM, at that time the world-dominant computing company. It would be impossibly expensive and counter-productive on an Elliott 803, with a word length of 39 bits, to give the same numerical answers as the IBM machine, which had only 36 bits in a word — we could more efficiently give greater accuracy and range. Even more unfair was the consequence that the IBM compiler was by definition correct; but any other manufacturer would be compelled to reproduce all of its errors — they would have to be called just anomalies, because errors would be logically impossible. Since then, I have always avoided operational approaches to programming-language semantics. The principle that "a program is what a program does" is not a good basis for exploration of the concept of program correctness.

I did not make a presentation at the Vienna conference, but I did make one comment: I thought that the most important attribute of a formal definition of semantics should be to leave certain aspects of the language carefully undefined. As a result, each implementation would have carefully circumscribed freedom to make efficient choices in the interests of its users and in the light of the characteristics of a particular machine architecture. I was very encouraged that this comment was applauded, and even Garwick expressed his agreement. In fact, I had mis-interpreted his title: his paper called for an abstract compiler for an abstract machine, rather than selection of an actual commercial product as standard.

The inspiration of my remark in Vienna dates back to 1952, when I went to Oxford as an undergraduate student. Some of my neighbours in College were mathematicians, and I joined them in a small unofficial night-time reading party to study Mathematical Logic from the textbook by Quine [9]. Later, a course in the philosophy of mathematics pursued more deeply this interest in axioms and proofs, as an explanation of the unreasonable degree of certainty which accompanies the contemplation of mathematical truth. It was this background that led me to propose the axiomatic method for defining the semantics of a programming language, while preserving a carefully controlled vagueness in certain aspects. I drew the analogy with the foundations of the various branches of mathematics, like projective geometry or group theory; each branch is in effect defined by the set of axioms that are used without further justification in all proofs of the theorems of that branch. The axioms are written in the common notations of mathematics, but they also contain a number of undefined terms, like lines and points in projective geometry, or units and products in group theory; these constitute the conceptual framework of that branch. I was convinced that an axiomatic presentation of the basic concepts of programming would be much simpler than any compiler of any language for any computer, however abstract.

I still believe that axioms provide an excellent interface between the roles of the pure mathematician and the applied mathematician. The pure mathematician deliberately gives no explicit meaning to the undefined terms appearing in the axioms, theorems, and proofs. It is the task of the applied mathematician and the experimental scientist to find in the real world a possible meaning for the terms, and check by carefully designed experiment that this meaning satisfies the axioms. The engineer is even allowed to take the axioms as a specification which must be met in the design of a product, for example, the compiler for a programming language. Then all the theorems for that branch of pure mathematics can be validly applied to the product, or to the relevant real-world domain. And surprisingly often, the more abstract approach of the pure mathematician is rewarded by the discovery that there are many different applications of the same axiom set. By analogy, there could be many different implementations of the axiom set which defines a standard programming language. That was exactly, the carefully circumscribed freedom that I wanted for the compiler writer, who has to take the normal engineer's responsibility that the implementation satisfies the axioms, as well as efficiently running its users' programs.

My first proposal for such an axiom set took the form of equations, as encountered in school texts on algebra, but with fragments of program on the left and right hand sides of the equation instead of numbers and numeric expressions. The same idea was explored earlier and more thoroughly in a doctoral dissertation by Shigeru Igarashi at the University of Tokyo [10]. In November 1967, I showed my first pencilled draft of a paper on the axiomatic approach to Peter Lucas; he was leading a project at the IBM Research Laboratory in Vienna to give a formal definition to IBM's new programming language, later known as PL/I [11]. He was attracted by the proposal, but he fairly soon abandoned the attempt to apply it to PL/I as a whole. The designers of PL/I had a very operational view of what each construct of the language would do, and they had no inclination to support a level of abstraction necessary for an attractive or helpful axiomatic presentation of the semantics. I was not disappointed: in the arrogance of idealism, I was confirmed in my view that a good formal definition method would be one that clearly reveals the quality of a programming language, whether bad or good; and the axiomatic method had shown its capability of at least revealing badness. Other evidence for the badness of PL/I was its propensity for crashing programs.

2. Research in Belfast, 1968–1977

By 1968, it was evident that research into programming language semantics was going to take a long time before it found application in industry; and in those days it was accepted that long-term research should take place in universities. I therefore welcomed the opportunity to take up a post as Professor of Computer Science at the Queen's University in Belfast. By a happy coincidence, as I was moving house, I came across a preprint of Robert Floyd's paper on Assigning Meanings to Programs [12]. Floyd adopted the same philosophy as I had, that the meaning of a programming language is defined by the rules that can be used for reasoning about programs in the language. These could include not only equations, but also rules of inference. By this means, he presented an effective method of proving the total correctness of programs, not just their equality to other programs. I saw this as the achievement of the ultimate goal of a good formal semantics for a good programming language, namely, the complete avoidance of programming error. Furthermore, the quality of the language was now the subject of objective scientific assessment, based on simplicity of the axioms and the guidance they give for program construction. The axiomatic method is a way to avoid the dogmatism and controversy that so often accompanies programming language design, particularly by committees.

For a general-purpose programming language, correctness can be defined only relative to the intention of a particular program. In many cases, the intention can be expressed as a post-condition of the program, that is an assertion about the values of the variables of the program that is intended to be true when the program terminates. The proof of this fact usually depends on annotating the program with additional assertions in the middle of the program text; these are expected to be true whenever execution of the program reaches the point where the assertion is written. At least one assertion, called an invariant, is needed in each loop: it is intended to be true before and after every execution of the body of the loop. Often, the correct working of a program depends on the assumption of some pre-condition, which must be true before the program starts. Floyd gave the proof rules whose application could guarantee the validity of all the assertions except the pre-condition, which had to be assumed. He even looked forward to the day when a verifying compiler could actually check the validity of all the assertions automatically before allowing the program to be run. This would be the ultimate solution to the problem of programming error, making it logically impossible in a running program; though I correctly predicted its achievement would be some time after, I had retired from academic life, which would be in 30 year's time.

I was even worried that my axiomatic method was too powerful, because it could deal with jumps, which Dijkstra had pointed out to be a bad feature of the conventional programming of the day [22]. My consolation was that the proof rule for jumps relies on a subsidiary hypothesis, and is inherently more complicated than the rules for structured programming constructs. Subsequent wide adoption of structured programming confirmed my view that simplicity of the relevant proof rule is an objective measure of quality in a programming language feature. Further confirmation is now provided by program analysis tools like Lint [23] and PREfix [24], applied to less disciplined languages such as C; they identify just those constructions that would invalidate the simple and obvious proof methods, and warn against their use.

A common objection to Floyd's method of program proving was the need to supply additional assertions at intermediate points in the program. It is very difficult to look at an existing program and guess what these assertions should be. I thought this was an entirely mistaken objection. It was not sensible to try to prove the correctness of existing programs, partly because they were mostly going to be incorrect anyway. I followed Dijkstra's constructive approach [25] to task of programming: the obligation of ultimate correctness should be the driving force in designing programs that were going to be correct by construction. In this top-down approach, the starting point for a software project should always be the specification, and the proof of the program should be developed along with the program itself. Thus, the most effective proofs are those constructed before the program is written. This philosophy has been beautifully illustrated in Dijkstra's own book on *A Discipline of Programming* [26], and in many subsequent textbooks on formal approaches to software engineering [27].

In all my work on the formalisation of proof methods for sequential programming languages, I knew that I was only preparing the way for a much more serious challenge, which was to extend the proof technology into the realm of concurrent program execution. In the early 1970s, I took as my first model of concurrency a kind of quasi-parallel programming (co-routines), which was introduced by Ole-Johan Dahl and Kristen Nygaard into Simula (and later Simula 67) for purposes of discrete event simulation [28, 29]. I knew the Simula concept of an object as a replicable structure of data, declared in a class together with the methods which are allowed to update its attributes. As an exercise in the application of these ideas, I took the structured implementation of a paging system (virtual memory). I suddenly realised that the purpose and criterion of correctness of the program was to simulate the more abstract concept of a single-level memory, with a much wider addressing range than could be physically fitted into the random access memory of the computer. The concept had to be represented in a complicated (but fortunately concealed) way, by storing temporarily unused data on a disk [30]. The correctness of the code could be proved with the aid of an invariant assertion, later known as the abstraction invariant, that connects the abstract variable to its concrete representation [31]. The introduction of such abstractions into programming practice is one of the main achievements of still current craze for object-oriented programming.

The real insight that I derived from this exercise was that exactly the same proof was valid, not only for sequential use of the virtual memory, but also for its use by many processes running concurrently. As in the case of proof-driven program development, it is the obligation of correctness that should drive the design of a good programming language feature. Of course, efficiency of implementation is also important. A correct implementation of the abstraction has to prevent more than one process from updating the concrete representation at the same time. This is efficiently done by use of Dijkstra's semaphores protecting critical regions [32]; the resulting structure was called a *monitor* [33, 34]. The idea was simultaneously put forward and successfully tested by Per Brinch Hansen in his efficient implementation of Concurrent PASCAL [35]. The monitor has since been adopted for the control of concurrency by the more recently fashionable language Java [36], but with extensions that prevent the use of the original simple proof rules.

To test the applicability of these ideas, I used them to design the structure of a simple batch processed operating system [37]. Jim Welsh and Dave Bustard implemented the system in an extended version of Pascal, called Pascal Plus, which they also designed and implemented [38]. We made extensive use on the **inner** statement of Simula 67, which enables the code of a user process to be embedded deep inside an envelope of code which implements the abstract resources that it uses. The same effect is achieved in object-oriented languages today by methods which initialise and finalise an object. In Simula, the semantics of the **inner** statement is described like that of the procedure call in ALGOL 60 (and inheritance in current object-oriented languages), in terms of textual copying of portions of the user program inside the code of the object which it is using. Dijkstra rightly pointed out to me that such a copy rule completely fails to explain or exploit the real merit of the language feature, which is to raise the level of abstraction of the program. So, we spent some time together at a Marktoberdorf Summer School, exploring the underlying abstraction, and to design notations that would most clearly express it. But it took several more years of personal research, and I was still not satisfied with my progress. Inspiration eventually came from an unexpected direction.

That was the time at which the promise of very large scale integration was beginning to be realised in the form of low-cost microprocessors. In order to multiply their somewhat modest computing power, it was an attractive prospect to connect several such machines by means of wires along which they could communicate with each other during program execution. To write programs for such an assembly of machines, a programming language would have to include input and output commands; these removed the need for an explanation by textual copying. The idea of sharing storage among microprocessors was ruled out by the expense, and without shared store, monitors are unnecessary. An obvious requirement for a parallel programming language is a means of connecting two program fragments in parallel, rather than in series. Naturally, I chose the structured parallel command (parbegin ... parend) suggested by Dijkstra [32], rather than the jump-like forking primitive made popular by C and UNIX. I also included a variant of Dijkstra's guarded command [39], to enable a program to reduce latency by waiting for the first of two (or more) inputs to become available. The resulting program structures were known as Communicating Sequential Processes [40]. To answer the question of the sufficiency of these few features, I showed that they could easily encode many other useful programming language constructions, both sequential and parallel. These included semaphores, subroutines, co-routines, and of course monitors.

I was very happy with the unification of programming concepts that I had achieved, but very dissatisfied that I had no means of proving the correctness of the programs that used them. Furthermore, there were a number of language design decisions which I left open, and which I wanted to resolve by investigating their impact on the ease of proving programs correct. I hoped that a Communicating Process could be understood in terms of the trace (or history) of all the communications in which it could engage. On this basis, I found it was possible to get proofs of partial correctness, but only by ignoring problems of non-termination and of non-deterministic deadlock, which causes a computer to stop when a cycle of processes are each waiting for its neighbour. I was by then ashamed that I had ignored such problems in my early exposition of Floyd's proof method. Fortunately, Dijkstra had shown in his Discipline of Programming [26] how to deal safely with the problem of non-determinism. He assumed that it would be resolved maliciously by a demon, intent on frustrating our intentions, whatever they might be. He also dealt correctly with the problem of non-termination. Now, I resolved that any acceptable proof method for CSP would have to incorporate Dijkstra's solutions.

3. Move to Oxford, 1977–1999

At that time, an opportunity arose to move to Oxford University, where I wanted to study the methods of denotational semantics that had been pioneered by Christopher Strachey and Dana Scott, and ably expounded in a more recent textbook by Joe Stoy [41]. Among my first research students, jointly supervised with Joe Stoy, were a couple of brilliant mathematicians, Bill Roscoe and Steve Brookes. We followed the suggestion of Robin Milner that the meaning of a concurrent program could be determined by the collection of tests that could be made on it. Following Karl Popper's criterion of falsification for the meaning of a scientific theory, Roscoe and Brookes concentrated on failures of these tests, with particular attention to the circumstances in which they could deadlock or fail to terminate. This led to the now standard model of CSP, with traces, refusals, and divergences [42, 43].

This research found remarkably early application in industry. Iain Barron, who had earlier worked for Elliott Brothers on the design of the 803 computer, was inspired by the vision of a new computer architecture, the *transputer*, which he defined as a complete microprocessor, communicating with its neighbours in a network by input and output along simple wires [44]. He started up a company called Inmos to design and make the hardware, he hired David May as its chief architect, and he hired me as a consultant on the design of a programming language based on CSP to control it. The language was named occam [45, 46], after the medieval Oxford philosopher, who proposed simplicity as the ultimate touchstone of truth.

An important commercial goal of the company was to ensure that the same parallel program would have logically the same effect when implemented by multi-programming on a single computer as when distributed over multiple processors on a network. The level of abstraction provided by CSP gave just this assurance. For 10 years or more, the transputer enjoyed commercial success and the language excited scientific interest; but today's advances in microprocessor power, storage capacity, and network communications technology favour a more dynamic model of network configuration and a buffered model of communication, which are more directly represented in more recent process algebras, like the *pi*-calculus [47].

Fundamental to the philosophy of top-down development of programs from their specifications is the ability of programmers to write the specifications in the first place. Obviously, these specifications have to be at least an order of magnitude simpler and more obviously correct than the eventual program is going to be. In the 1980s, it was accepted wisdom that the language for writing specifications should itself be executable, making it, in effect, just another more powerful programming language. But, I knew that in principle a language like that of set theory, untrammelled by considerations of execution (or of efficiency), could express many important abstract concepts far more concisely than any executable language; and I believed that these concepts drawn from mathematics would make it easier to reason about the correctness of the program at the design stage. There is no conceivable way of proving a specification correct (against what specification would that be? Such a higher-level specification, if it existed, should have been chosen originally as the starting place for the design). So, the only hope is to make the original specification so clear and so easily understandable that it obviously describes what is wanted, and not some other thing. That is why it would be dangerous to recommend for specification anything less than the full language of mathematics. Even if this view is impractical, it represents the kind of extreme in expressive power that makes it an appropriate topic for academic research. Certainly, if the basic mathematical concepts turn out to be inadequate to describe what is wanted, there is little hope for help from mathematics in making correct programs.

Mathematicians through the ages have developed a great many notations, and each branch of the subject uses the same notations for different purposes, and unfortunately different notations for the same purpose. What is needed for purposes of programming is a uniform notational framework to match the generality of a general-purpose programming language, and sufficiently powerful for the definition of all concepts of any particular branch of mathematics that might be relevant to any computer application in the future. Fortunately, this was provided by abstract set theory, developed as a foundation for mathematics by logicians at the beginning of the last century. Set theory already provides a range of concepts known to be relevant in computing — Cartesian products, direct sums, trees, sequences, bags, sets, functions, and relations. The same idea had inspired Jean-Raymond Abrial, a successful French software engineer; and he came to Oxford in the early eighties to continue his work on the Z specification language [48]. The power of the Z notation was first tested by researchers at Oxford, working on small tutorial examples; and many improvements resulted, both in notation and style of usage. But the crucial question was: would they provide any practical benefit when applied to a large programming project in industry?

At that time, the IBM development laboratories in Hursley were supporting our research in Oxford, both financially and scientifically, in a project led by Ib Sorensen and Ian Hayes. One of their teams was responsible for the development of the Customer Information and Control System CICS, one of their most successful commercial software products; and they were planning the next release of this system, primarily devoted to the re-structuring of some of its basic components. For one of the more tricky components, they bravely decided to try our new recommended top-down development method, starting with a specification in Z. This involved more work in the early stages of the project, but it gave good confidence in the soundness of the design of the new structure; and the early rigorous formalisation averted many errors that might have been troublesome at later stages in the project. In the end, the development costs, even on first use of Z, were less than on components developed in the traditional way, and the quality as perceived by the customer was greater [49].

The characteristic feature of Z is the *schema*, consisting of a declaration of the names of certain free variables and their types, together with a predicate expressing a desired invariant relationship between the values of those variables. The free variables play the same role as in a scientific theory: they stand for measurements like time and distance that can be made in the real world, or (in our application) they stand for observations of the state or behaviour of computer programs. The meanings of the variables, and the justification for the invariants, must be described informally in the extremely important natural-language prose that accompanies the specification. As in science, there are many common conventions: so in a schema that specifies a fragment of a sequential program, a dashed variable x' always stands for the final value of a global program variable whose initial value is denoted by x. It was Cliff Jones, a leader in the development of the Vienna Development Method (VDM), who persuaded me of the need to make explicit both initial and final values of all the variables [50].

The extra flexibility of these extra variables makes it easy to introduce extensions to the model of a programming language. For example, to model timing properties, just introduce a special real-valued variable called *time*. So *time'* would be the time at which a program terminates, and *time* would be when it starts. Of course, the programmer is not allowed to assign arbitrary values to such a special variable. It can be updated only by special operations like *delay (interval)*, whose effect is simply modelled by adding the *interval* to the *time*; though the intended implementation is also rather special: just wait for the clock on the wall to move on. Such extra variables played a vital role in my later attempts at unifying theories of programming.

Like predicates in logic, Z schemas can be connected by any of the operators of the propositional calculus: conjunction, disjunction, and even negation. But the schema calculus also uses sequential composition; which is defined in the same way as the binary composition of relations in relational calculus. The final values of the variables of the first program (before the semicolon) are identified with the initial values of the second program (after the semicolon), and these intermediate values are hidden by existential quantification. A careful treatment of non-termination ensures that the composition of two schemas accurately describes the result of sequential execution of any pair of programs which satisfy those schemas. More formally, if $P1$ and $P2$ are programs, and if $S1$ and $S2$ are schemas, then the axiomatic proof rule for correctness of sequential composition of programs can be elegantly expressed:

$$\frac{P1 \text{ satisfies } S1 \quad P2 \text{ satisfies } S2}{(P1; P2) \text{ satisfies } (S1; S2)}$$

One day in the middle of 1981, Rick Hehner, on a sabbatical visit to Oxford, came into my office and spent an embarrassingly long time persuading me that something much simpler was possible [51, 52]. Just define the semantics of the programming language directly in terms of the schema calculus of Z. Each program is interpreted as the strongest schema describing its observable behaviour on all its possible executions. As a result, the concept of satisfaction of a specification can be identified with the most pervasive concept in all mathematical reasoning, that of logical implication. Furthermore, there is no need any longer for an axiomatic semantics, because all the useful proof rules can themselves be proved as theorems. All the operators of the programming language are defined simply as operators on schemas. For example, the definition of semicolon in the programming language is identical to its definition given above in the schema calculus. The proof rule displayed above is no longer an axiom; it is a proven theorem stating the simple fact that relational composition is monotonic in both its operands, with respect to implication ordering. For the next 10 years, I travelled the world giving a series of keynote addresses with different illustrative examples, but with the same message and the same title: Programs are Predicates [53–55].

The first application of this wonderful insight was to solve the long-standing problem of the specification and proof of correctness of Communicating Sequential Processes. All that is needed is to introduce the observable attributes of a process, its *trace* and its *refusals*, as free variables of a Z schema. Then, the various choice and parallel constructions of CSP are defined using predicate calculus as operators on schemas. This insight has inspired all my subsequent research. In a continuing collaboration with He Jifeng, we have developed a specification-oriented semantics for many other computational paradigms, including hardware and software, declarative and procedural, sequential and parallel. Even within parallel programming, there are many variations, some with distributed processing some with shared store, with dedicated channels or with shared buses, with synchronised or with buffered communication. It turns out that there is much in common between the mathematical properties of all the paradigms; and this led us to describe our activity as Unifying Theories of Programming [56]. This work brought to fruition a strand of my research that was started by Peter Lauer, my first successful doctoral student in Belfast [57].

That concludes a brief account of my long research association with assertions. They started as simple Boolean expressions in a sequential programming language, testing a property of a single machine state at the point that control reaches the assertion. By adding dashed variables to stand for the values of variables at the termination of the program, an assertion is generalised to a complete specification of an arbitrary fragment of a sequential program. By adding variables that record the history of interactions between a program and its environment, assertions specify the interfaces between concurrent programs. By defining the semantics of a program as the strongest assertion that describes all its possible behaviours, we give a complete method for proving the total correctness of all programs expressed in the language. My interest in assertions was triggered by problems that I had encountered as a programmer in industry. The evolution of the idea kept me occupied throughout my academic career. Now on return to industrial employment, I have the opportunity to see how the idea has progressed towards practical application, and maybe help to progress it a bit further.

4. Back in Industry, 1999

The contrast between my academic research and current software engineering practice in industry could not be more striking. A programmer working on legacy code in industry rarely has the privilege of starting again from scratch. If a specification is provided, it is usually no more than the instruction "do something useful and attractive, making as little change as possible in the existing code base or its behaviour". The details of the design are largely determined by what turns out to be possible and adequately efficient after exploration of the existing code and testing a number of possible changes by experiment. The only way of improving the correctness of the result is by debugging. The practice of specification of an interface even as simple as a histogram graphics package is quite unattractive, and formal proof is clearly inconceivable on existing code bases, measured in millions of lines of code. So, how can the results of theoretical research, inspired by purely academic ideals, be brought to bear on the pervasive problems of maintaining large-scale legacy code written in legacy languages?

It is the concept of an assertion that links my earlier research with current industrial software engineering practice, and provides the basis for hopes of future improvement. Assertions figure very strongly in Microsoft code. A recent count discovered over quarter of a million of them in the code for Office. The primary role of an assertion today is as a test oracle, defining the circumstances under which a program under test is considered to fail. A collection of aptly placed assertions is what permits a massive suite of test cases to be run overnight, in the absence of human intervention. Failure of an assertion triggers a dump of the program state, to be analysed by the programmer on the following morning. Apart from merely indicating the fact of failure, the place where the first assertion fails is likely to give a good indication of where and why the program is going wrong. And this indication is given in advance of any crash, so avoiding the risk that the necessary diagnostic information is over-written. So assertions have already found their major application, not to the proof of the correctness of programs, but to the diagnosis of their errors. They are applied as a partial solution to the problems of program crashes, which I first encountered as a new programmer in 1960. The other solution is the ubiquitous personal work-station, which reduces the turn-round for program correction from days to minutes.

Assertions are usually compiled differently for test runs and for code that is shipped to the customer. In ship code, the assertions are often omitted, to avoid the run-time penalty and the confusion that would follow from an error diagnostic or a checkpoint dump in view of the customer. Ideally, the only assertions to be omitted are those that have been subjected to proof. But more practically, many teams leave the assertions in ship code to generate an exception when false; to continue execution in such an unexpected and untested circumstance would run a grave risk of crash. So instead, the handler for the exception makes a recovery that is sensible to the customer in the environment of use.

Assertions are also used to advantage by program analysis tools like PREfix [23]; this is being developed within Microsoft, for application to the maintenance of legacy code. The value of such tools is limited if they give so many warning messages that the programmer cannot afford the time to examine them. Ideally, each warning should be accompanied by an automatically generated test case that would reveal the bug; but that will depend on further advances in model checking and theorem proving. Assertions and assumptions provide a means for the programmer to explain that a certain error cannot occur, or is irrelevant, and the tool will suppress the corresponding sheaf of error reports. This is another motivating factor for programmers to include more and stronger assertions in their code. Another acknowledged motive is to inform programmers engaged in subsequent program modification that certain properties of the program must be maintained.

My work with Microsoft concentrates on further design and development of tools to assist in the programming of trustworthy systems and applications. In other engineering disciplines, design automation tools embody an increasing amount of scientific knowledge, mathematical calculations, and engineering know-how. My hope is that similar tools will lead the way in delivering the results of research into programming theory to the working software engineer, even to one who is working primarily on legacy code. I suggest that assertional proof principles should define the direction of evolution of sophisticated program analysis tools. Without principles, a program analysis tool has to depend only on heuristics, and after a time, further advance becomes increasingly difficult. There is the danger that programmers can learn to write code that has all the characteristics of good style as defined by the heuristics, and yet be full of bugs. The only principles that guard against this risk are those which are directly based on considerations of program correctness. And that is why program correctness has been, and still remains, a suitable topic for academic research.

References

[1] *Elliott 803 Programming Manual* (Elliott Brothers (London) Ltd., Borehamwood, Herts, 1960).

[2] D. Shell, A high-speed sorting procedure, *Comm. ACM* **2** (1959) 30–32.

[3] P. Naur (ed), Report on the algorithmic language ALGOL 60, *Comm. ACM* **3**(5) (1960) 299–314.

[4] N. Chomsky, *Syntactic Structures* (Mouton & Co., The Hague, 1957).

[5] J. W. Backus, The syntax and the semantics of the proposed international algebraic language of the Zurich ACM-GAMM conference, *ICIP Proceedings, Paris*, 1959, pp. 125–132.

[6] T. Hoare, Report on the Elliott ALGOL translator, *Comp. J.* **5**(4) (1963) 345–348.

[7] T. B. Steel Jr. ed., *Formal Language Description Languages for Computer Programming* (North Holland, Amsterdam 1966).

[8] Jan V. Garwick, The definition of programming languages by their compilers *ibid.*

[9] W. V. O. Quine, *Mathematical Logic*. Revised edition (Harvard University Press, 1955).

[10] S. Igarashi, An axiomatic approach to equivalence problems of algorithms with applications. PhD Thesis, Tokyo University, 1964.

[11] P. Lucas, *et al.*, Informal introduction to the abstract syntax and interpretation of PL/I, ULD version II, IBM TR 25.03 (1968).

[12] R. W. Floyd, Assigning meanings to programs, *Proc. Am. Soc. Symp. Appl. Math.* **19** (1967) 19–31.

[13] T. Hoare, An axiomatic basis for computer programming, *Comm. ACM.* **12**(10) (1969) 576–580, 583.

[14] T. Hoare, *Procedures and Parameters: An Axiomatic Approach*, LNM 188. (Springer Verlag, Berlin, 1971).

[15] T. Hoare and M. Foley, Proof of a recursive program: QUICKSORT, *Comput. J.* **14** (1971) 391–395.

[16] T. Hoare, Towards a theory of parallel programming, in *Operating Systems Techniques*, (Academic Press, 1972).

[17] T. Hoare and M. Clint, Program proving: jumps and functions, *Acta Inform.* **1** (1972) 214–224.

[18] T. Hoare, A note on the **for** statement, *BIT* **12**(3) (1972) 334–341.

[19] T. Hoare and N. Wirth, An axiomatic definition of the programming language PASCAL, *Acta Inform.* **2**(4) (1973) 335–355.

[20] R. L. London, *et al.*, Proof rules for the programming language EUCLID, *Acta Inform.* **10** (1978) 1–26.

[21] B. Meyer, *Object-Oriented Software Construction* (2nd ed.), (Prentice Hall PTR, 1997).

[22] E. W. Dijkstra, Go to statement considered harmful, *Comm. ACM* **11** (1968) 147–148.

[23] W. R. Bush, J. D. Pincus and D. J. Sielaff, A static analyser for finding dynamic programming errors, *Software Practice and Experience* **30** (2000) 775–802.

[24] S. C. Johnson, Lint: a C program checker, *UNIX Prog. Man. 4.2* UC (Berkeley, 1984).

[25] E. W. Dijkstra, A constructive approach to the problem of program correctness, *BIT* **8** (1968) 174–186.

[26] E. W. Dijkstra, *A Discipline of Programming* (Prentice Hall, 1976).

[27] C. Morgan, *Programming from Specifications* (Prentice Hall International, 1990).

[28] O.-J. Dahl, *et al.*, SIMULA 67 common base language, *Norwegian Computer Centre* (1967).

[29] O.-J. Dahl and T. Hoare, Hierarchical program structures, in *Structured Programming*, (Academic Press, 1972) 175–220.

[30] T. Hoare, A structured paging system, *Comp. J.* **16**(3) (1973) 209–215.

[31] T. Hoare, Proof of correctness of data representations, *Acta Inform.* **1**(4) (1972) 271–281.

[32] E. W. Dijkstra, Cooperating sequential processes, in *Programming Languages*, ed. F. Genuys, (Academic Press, New York, 1968) 43–112.

[33] P. Brinch Hansen, Structured multiprogramming, *Comm. ACM* **15**(7) (1972) 574–578.

[34] T. Hoare, Monitors: an operating system structuring concept, *Comm. ACM* **17**(10) (1974) 549–557.

[35] P. Brinch Hansen, The programming language concurrent Pascal, *IEEE Trans. Soft. Eng.* **1**(2) (1975) 199–207.

[36] J. Gosling, W. Joy and G. Steel, *The Java Language Specification* (Addison-Wesley, 1996).

[37] T. Hoare, The structure of an operating system, in *Springer LNCS* **46** (1976) 242–265.

[38] J. Welsh and D. Bustard, *Concurrent Program Structures* (Prentice Hall International, 1988).

[39] E. W. Dijkstra, Guarded commands, non-determinacy, and the formal derivation of programs, *Comm. ACM* **18** (1975) 453–457.

[40] T. Hoare, Communicating sequential processes, *Comm. ACM* **21**(8) (1978) 666–777.

[41] J. Stoy, *Denotational Semantics, The Scott-Strachey Approach to Programming Language Theory* (MIT Press, 1977).

[42] S. Brookes and A. W. Roscoe, An improved failures model for CSP, in *Springer LNCS* **197** (1985).

[43] T. Hoare, *Communicating Sequential Processes* (Prentice Hall International, 1985).

[44] INMOS Limited, *Transputer Reference Manual* (Prentice Hall International, 1988).

[45] T. Hoare, The transputer and occam: a personal story, *Conc. Pract. and Exp.* **3**(4) (1991) 249–264.

[46] G. Jones and M. Goldsmith, *Programming in Occam 2* (Prentice Hall International, 1989).

[47] R. Milner, *Communicating and Mobile Systems: The Pi-Calculus* (Cambridge University Press, 1999).

[48] J.-R. Abrial, Assigning programs to meanings, in *Mathematical Logic and Programming Languages*, Philosophical Transactions of the Royal Society, Series A, Vol 31 (1984).

[49] B. P. Collins, J. E. Nicholls and I. H. Sorensen, Introducing formal methods, *The CICS Experience*, IBM TR 260 (Hursley Park, Winchester, 1989).

[50] C. B. Jones, Software development, in *A Rigorous Approach* (Prentice Hall International, 1980).

[51] E. C. R. Hehner, Predicative programming, *Comm. ACM* **27**(2) (1984).

[52] T. Hoare and E. C. R. Hehner, A more complete model of communicating processes, *Theor. Comp. Sci.* **26**(1&2) (1983) 105–120.

[53] T. Hoare and A. W. Roscoe, Programs as executable predicates, in *Proceedings of the International Conference on Fifth Generation Computer Systems*, Tokyo, ICOT, 1984, pp. 220–228.

[54] T. Hoare, Programs are predicates, in *Mathematical Logic and Programming Languages*, Phil Trans. Royal Soc. Ser. A Vol 31 (1984).

[55]   T. Hoare, Programs are predicates, *New Gen. Comp.* **38** (1993) 2–15.
[56]   T. Hoare and He Jifeng, *Unifying Theories of Programming* (Prentice Hall International, 1998).
[57]   T. Hoare and P. E. Lauer, Consistent and complementary formal theories of the semantics of programming languages, *Acta Inform.* **3**(2) (1974) 135–153.

Chapter 6

THE CALL TO ARMs

STEVE FURBER

ICL Professor of Computer Engineering
School of Computer Science
The University of Manchester
Oxford Road, Manchester M13 9PL, UK
steve.furber@manchester.ac.uk

By the end of 2007, more than 10,000,000,000 ARM processors had been manufactured, making the ARM the highest volume processor in the 32-and-above-bit space of all time, by a very large margin. The origins of the ARM can be traced back to a small UK supplier of desk-top machines, Acorn Computer Ltd, in the early 1980s, for whose staff the original ARM (then the "Acorn RISC Machine") was a first attempt at designing a microprocessor. The ultimate success of the ARM is a result of serendipity (of course) combined with a little good technical judgement, a great deal of creativity in developing a novel business model, and a focus on customer service. The technical development of the ARM has as its foundations some of the important developments in computer science over the last quarter of a century: its architectural conception was a result of skillful selling of the RISC philosophy by its exponents at Berkeley; its silicon design employed very early design automation tools; its simplicity, small size and power-efficiency suited it to the emerging System-on-Chip (SoC) technology of the early 1990s, and its foothold there enabled it to climb into its dominant position in the consumer technology of the digital age — the pervasive mobile multimedia communications appliances of the early 21st century. This chapter will principally cover the early period of ARM history, during the 1980s, before the ARM emerged onto the world stage under the management of the company that bears its name.

1. Acorn Computer Ltd

The company that begat the ARM started sometime around 1978. Chris Curry (ex-Sinclair Radionics, then running Science of Cambridge) and Hermann Hauser (then at the University of Cambridge Cavendish laboratory) decided to pursue their interest in microcomputers and formed CPU (Cambridge Processor Unit) Limited. CPU Ltd first carried out consultancy work on microprocessor-based controllers for fruit machines, but when Sophie Wilson went home from university one Easter and came back with a design for a small 6502-based microcomputer system (inspired by, though in no way based upon, the Science of Cambridge SC/MP-based MK14 product) Curry and Hauser decided to market Wilson's design as the Acorn Microcomputer (later renamed the Acorn System 1), introducing the Acorn name for trading purposes to avoid confusion with the consultancy business. It did not go unnoticed that Acorn comes before Apple in the phone book!

The timing for the Acorn Microcomputer was good as public interest in microprocessors was growing rapidly. Over the next year or two, the company's focus moved away from consultancy to selling the System 1 and its successors, and the company changed its name to Acorn Computer Limited. It was based at 4a, Market Hill, in the centre of Cambridge, in rather un-prepossessing offices above the electricity board showrooms which faced the market. The approach, through a narrow passage to the side of the shop, was particularly popular with the local pigeons!

The Acorn System 1 comprised two standard 100 mm by 160 mm "Eurocard" printed circuit boards (PCBs), one of which was dominated by the LED display and hexadecimal keypad, the other incorporating the 6502 microprocessor and most of the other electronics. The system could be used stand-alone, but the processor card could also be configured for plugging into a 19-inch rack, and Acorn developed a range of cards that could be plugged into the rack with it — floppy disk drive controllers, display controllers, analogue-digital converters, and so on. Various rack-mounted configurations were sold as the System 2 and 3. These were adaptable and suited to various industrial control applications, but the rack system was expensive. To bring a higher specification product to the consumer market required a different approach.

By this time the Apple II was well-established in the United States, and this showed the way forward from the hexadecimal-keypad-and-display bare PCB system. Acorn developed the Atom product, again based on the 6502, but now incorporating a full typewriter-style keyboard and an output to drive a display monitor or TV. The display driver generated a 60 Hz (US-standard) frame rate picture, which was a bit of a problem in the UK where the standard is 50 Hz, but this was survivable and the Atom sold well. Initially, the Atom was sold in kit form (as had the System 1), but the market for microprocessor products was expanding beyond those enthusiasts who knew which end to hold a soldering iron. After a number of kits had been returned with constructional faults (the most extreme of which was the machine whose chips had been glued-in to avoid the risk of heat damage from soldering!) the company increasingly sold fully-manufactured products.

The Atom introduced a number of innovations to the UK market, including low-cost computer networking — the Acorn Econet.

To build on the success of the Atom, Acorn began to look at possible successor products, and surveyed what might succeed the 6502 as the core microprocessor around which such a system might be based. Various 16-bit microprocessors were investigated. One plan, which was known internally as the Proton, was a dual-processor system that used a 6502 as a front-end IO processor together with an unspecified 16-bit processor that ran the application code. This design was on the drawing board together when the company got wind of the BBC's plans.

2. The BBC Micro

In 1980, the BBC had conceived the idea of basing a computer literacy series around a specific machine, but the machine they planned to use was not progressing well. They were persuaded to visit Acorn early in 1981, and Acorn planned to use the front-end of the Proton as their offering. The full dual-processor Proton was too expensive, although the second processor interface would be retained for future expansion. With a week's notice of the visit, the company planned to do what it could to impress them. Allen Boothroyd was asked to mock up a case design, and Hermann Hauser played one of his legendary games with the technical team. During the weekend before the BBC's visit (which was on the following Friday) he rang Sophie Wilson asking if a prototype could be built for the visit. All we had at that time was a rough paper sketch of the Proton circuit. Wilson did not think there was enough time. Hermann then rang me with the same question, saying Wilson thought it could be done. I was doubtful, but agreed that if Wilson thought it could be done I would give it a go, so he then rang Wilson again, this time saying that I thought it could be done, and Wilson also agreed. I fleshed out the circuit diagram, Ram Banerjee (the fastest [wire-wrap] gun in the west!) spent from Monday to Wednesday wire-wrapping the prototype, then a 24-hour-a-day debugging process yielded a working system at 7 am on the Friday morning. When the BBC arrived mid-morning BASIC was running, and by the afternoon some graphics could be displayed.

The BBC was duly impressed by the working prototype, the case model, and generally by Acorn's ability to move quickly, and Acorn was awarded the contract to develop the BBC Microcomputer. The design was refined and put into production between Easter 1981 and the end of the same year, and shipped in January 1982. The early forecasts of up to 12,000 sales proved hopelessly wrong, and Acorn struggled to keep up with demand for several years, with over 1.5 million Beebs produced in total. The Beeb provided the computing resource for most of the UK education system through the 1980s and found many other markets in universities (sometimes just as a cheap dumb terminal), in homes, and overseas.

3. Why Design a Microprocessor?

The BBC Micro was a major technical as well as a commercial success. Enormous technical risks were taken in its design, such as the use of very early gate arrays (Ferranti ULAs — Uncommitted Logic Arrays) to reduce the chip count, the use of telesoftware downloads (exploiting unused lines in the teletext content of broadcast TV pictures), 2nd processors, and so on. All of these paid-off (though not without some difficulty in certain cases), and the young and somewhat inexperienced technical team grew in confidence, perhaps even arrogance? Everything we touched seemed to turn to gold (though not much of that ended up in our pockets thanks to a certain naivety regarding financial matters). So, when we came to address the issue of the next machine to build on the success of the BBC Micro all options were open.

At that time we knew how to put chips together on a PCB, and we had solid experience of Ferranti's ULA technology, so we knew a bit about gate-array-level chip design. But microprocessors were a black art practised only by the big semiconductor companies, and even then they took several expensive iterations to get designs right. We visited the National Semiconductor 16032 (later renamed the 32016) design team in Israel, who were on the 6th or 7th revision of the processor and it still had bugs. We heard similar stories from elsewhere — this was clearly not a game that a small-system company could play.

However, the 16-bit processors that were being produced in the early 1980s did not impress us. On the whole their design was derivative, reflecting what had been best practice in minicomputers in the late 1970s (when the VAX 11/780 was king). In particular, two features of these processors disappointed us:

- they had very complex, uninterruptible instructions, which compromised the interrupt latency. The BBC Micro did all of its IO on interrupts, but the 16-bit processors had a worse interrupt performance than the Beeb's 6502. This did not seem like progress!
- worse still, the new 16-bit processors did not perform very well. We had looked at what determined processor performance and worked out that, above all, it was the processor's ability to exploit memory bandwidth that mattered. These 16-bit processors could not exploit the full bandwidth available from commodity memories at the time — indeed, they were no faster than the contemporary high clock rate 8-bit processors. A 4 MHz 6502 could outrun a 6 MHz 16032, and despite the "primitive" 8-bit instruction set of the 6502 and the "nice" instruction set of the 16032, the performance seemed to correlate only with the useful memory bandwidth.

Then (this is now 1983) we heard about the Berkeley work, and in particular "The Case for the Reduced Instruction Set Computer" [1], and everything started to fall into place. If a class of postgraduate students could design a competitive microprocessor in a year the task could not be so much of a black art as we had previously believed.

Alongside this thinking, the Acorn management (and in particular Hermann Hauser) had looked at developments in the industry and had concluded that "in the future there will only be two sorts of computer company: those that have learnt to design on silicon, and those that have gone out of business". On the basis of this insight alone, and with no idea as to how they might be used, Acorn had started to recruit experienced chip designers, bought Apollo workstations, and acquired VLSI design software from VLSI Technology, Inc., a company with whom Acorn had already established a business relationship as a result of them second-sourcing NMOS replacements for some of the Ferranti ULAs in Acorn's products.

Thus, in 1983, Sophie Wilson began to design an instruction set for a new microprocessor. At this time we were far from convinced that designing our own microprocessor was sensible, but we thought we would set out down this path, expecting at any point to discover where the roadblock lay. At that point we would abandon the project, but would have gained knowledge with which we could return to the job of sourcing a commercial processor.

The final experience that launched the project was a visit I made with Sophie Wilson to Phoenix, Arizona, in October 1983. We went to observe progress on the 65C816, an extended version of the 6502 with a 24-bit address space. What we found took us by surprise. The Western Design Centre, who were responsible for this design, were set up in a normal residential bungalow and employed school kids during the summer vacation to do the silicon layout of basic logic gates using ordinary Apple II computers. Sure, there were a few big bits of kit lying around for plotting large layouts and the like, but there were no deep mysteries in what we saw. If these guys could design a microprocessor then so could we.

It was time to go back to Cambridge and to talk Hermann into putting the project onto an official footing.

4. The ARM Design Process

In the early 1980s RISC was a new idea, espoused only by a few academic teams, and disdained by industry. The thrust towards simplicity that is implicit in the RISC philosophy was clearly a key to Acorn designing its own processor, with the very limited resources it could afford to apply to the job, but there was the fear that the academic instruction set architectures might have taken this a bit too far. Also, the Berkeley RISC design confused the picture somewhat with its register windows architecture which, although it has some clear benefits, also has drawbacks in terms of cost and context switching performance.

So there were debates about load-store architectures, the need for load-store multiple register instructions, conditional execution, and so on. I do not recall all of the issues, but Sophie Wilson was very firmly in control of the ISA definition. In the end the result was near-RISC, with a load-store architecture, a (fairly) large (almost) regular register file arrangement, (mainly) 3-address instructions, very powerful instructions for loading and storing multiple register, all instructions conditionally executed, and so on — very much the core of the ISA that is still in use today. Wilson's considerable experience in writing software — especially at that time BASIC interpreters — ensured that the ISA would support software efficiently.

Wilson also wrote an instruction set emulator so that the software team could develop and test ARM programs before any silicon became available. In particular, they developed validation programs — programs that test a particular aspect of the instruction set as exhaustively as possible — that were used to check out the ARM reference model that was the central component of the microarchitecture design.

The hardware design philosophy was based on the observation noted above — that memory bandwidth is the primary determinant of processor performance. Therefore, the ARM microarchitecture started from the idea that the processor clock would be tied to the memory clock, and the processor would use the memory for something (instruction fetch or data load or store) during every clock cycle. In order not to compromise the memory clock rate, the processor should deliver an address as early as possible in the clock cycle — possibly slightly before the start of the cycle if the memory allowed — and it would expect data to be returned as late as possible in the cycle. For cost reasons, the architecture would use a single memory with a single port, so the performance should be defined by the total number of memory accesses and the memory cycle time.

At that time commodity memory used DRAM chips that would deliver around 4 million random accesses per second, but in "page" mode they could operate at twice this rate. Page mode is restricted to addresses within the same row in the DRAM memory, but can readily be exploited when the processor is fetching instructions from consecutive memory locations, or performing any pattern of sequential accesses such as those that arise in a load or store multiple instruction, provided a test is made to detect the end-of-row.

A quick sum suggested that a 32-bit DRAM memory with around 75% sequential accesses would deliver approximately 25 Mbytes/s of bandwidth. The BBC Micro provided the 6502 processor with 2 Mbytes/s of memory bandwidth (plus another 2 Mbyte/s for the graphics), so if an ARM could make good use of 25 Mbyte/s it would deliver more than an order of magnitude performance improvement over a BBC Micro, and would significantly outperform any other microprocessor available at that time.

The microarchitecture design began from the objective of delivering this 25 Mbyte/s of usable bandwidth. The data-processing instructions required external memory only for instruction fetch, so it was necessary to be able to fetch an instruction in every clock cycle, implying some sort of pipelined execution (which was not a common feature of early 1980s microprocessors, though it had been used on the academic RISC prototypes whose protagonists declared it a better use of silicon resource than a complex micro-coded instruction set). After a little thought a Fetch-Decode-Execute pipeline was chosen as the simplest microarchitecture that could keep up with the memory.

Mapping the instruction set onto the processor datapath was a process of trial-and-error. Various datapath organisations were sketched, and replicated by photocopying. Then, for each clock cycle of each instruction, a sheet was coloured-in to indicate the datapath resource usage. If a conflict arose that seemed to cause the processor to take more than the ideal number of clock cycles to complete an instruction the datapath organisation was modified, replicated, and the colouring-in started again.

Then the ARM reference model was written. This was an 800-line program written in BBC Basic, using 32-bit integers to represent 32-bit data values. Each block (of which there were 20 or so, representing, for example, the instruction decoder PLA, the ALU or the instruction pipeline) was described using two subroutines, one of which was called in phase 1 of the clock and the other in phase 2. The 2-phase non-overlapping clock scheme was a fairly common design style for custom VLSI at the time [2] — one clock cycle comprised a phase 1 clock pulse followed by a phase 2 clock pulse, each clock phase controlling its own set of transparent latches — and allowed the control of race conditions by adjusting the non-overlap from outside the chip.

The ARM reference model ran the validation programs that had previously been developed and debugged using the instruction set emulator, and these were used to debug the reference model. Then the reference model function was documented in the form of block specifications — formal documents (of only a page or two each) that defined the function of each of the blocks that made up the processor. The block specs were the formal interface between the microarchitecture design and the VLSI design group, who each took responsibility for taking a number of blocks and generating schematics, layout and tests for them. The blocks were assembled into the complete chip layout, which was then tested, checked and made ready for fabrication.

The complete chip design was taken to VLSI Technology, Inc.'s offices in Munich early in January 1985, for final checks before tape-out — shipping the physical layout design files to the foundry for manufacture. The first silicon arrived on April 26, 1985, and at about 3 o'clock in the afternoon it was running BBC Basic.

There was a minor bug in an obscure corner of the shifter logic, but nothing of any real consequence. ARM1 was a working, usable processor that was faster than any on the market at that time, and the first commercial RISC microprocessor [3]. It would take a couple of years to complete the design of the full chip set, which included highly integrated memory, IO and video controllers to accompany the ARM, during which time a second iteration of the processor would be designed on a smaller (2 micron) CMOS process.

5. The Formation of ARM Ltd

In 1987, the ARM chip set formed the hardware basis for the Acorn Archimedes personal desk-top computers. These machines were well ahead of their time in performance terms, but the development of the sophisticated software that was required to exploit the hardware had suffered some setbacks. As a result, the first Archimedes machines were sold with rather inadequate software, somewhat compensated for by a reasonable backwards compatibility with the BBC Micro (which by then enjoyed a very substantial software base).

Acorn continued to develop the Archimedes system software which, unusually for the time, was delivered in ROMs (giving the machine extremely good start-up characteristics), but the IBM PC had established a standard throughout most of the desktop computing market that was hard for Acorn to compete with. Sales kept Acorn viable for a time, but there was no sign of the exponential growth that the company had enjoyed during the heyday of the BBC Micro, and maintaining a competitive position with a proprietary microprocessor was an increasingly expensive business. At the end of the 1980s, Acorn was looking for a way to relieve its balance sheet of the overhead of ARM development.

At the same time, Apple had a vision for the next generation of hand-held devices and was working on what would become the Newton. Their early developments were based around the AT&T Hobbit microprocessor, but they were reviewing this decision and approached Acorn to see if they could access the ARM under suitable conditions. One condition was that the ARM would be spun-out of Acorn into a new joint-venture company. They were pushing on an open door, and ARM Limited (the acronym expansion was first adjusted to "Advanced RISC Machine" and then later dropped altogether) was formed in November 1990.

The new company was formed around the ex-Acorn hardware and VLSI design teams (apart from me — I left to take up the ICL Chair in Computer Engineering at the University of Manchester in August 1990), the ARM technology, and was a joint venture of Apple, Acorn and VLSI Technology.

Robin Saxby was brought in as CEO, and devised the business model based on an up front fee to become an ARM partner (together with a royalty per manufactured chip) that generated positive cash flow and enabled the company to bootstrap itself effectively with no further investment beyond the small amounts provided by the founding parent companies.

ARM Ltd found itself ideally positioned to exploit the emerging SoC market of the early 1990s. After a bit of a struggle to break loose from the demands of the founding partners, it found the small size and low power of the ARM processor ideally suited to the needs of that time, when silicon resource was much more restricted than it is today and a small processor core left significantly more room for the remaining SoC components.

Throughout the 1990s, ARM Ltd focussed on simplifying the job of designing the ARM into an SoC. Debugging a complex system on a PCB is a hard job. Debugging a complex system inside a chip is about as difficult an engineering task as you will meet as everything has to be inferred from evidence that is available at the periphery through the pins, and chips are always designed to have as few pins as possible to minimise packaging costs. The original 3-stage ARM pipeline was augmented with on-chip debug resources, the compressed "Thumb" instruction set (to reduce code size by 30%), faster multipliers, and so on [4]. From the mid 1990s, new pipeline structures were developed to allow the architecture to address higher-end applications, complementing rather than replacing the simpler basic model. The major breakthrough came with the rapidly growing market for mobile-phone handsets, which ARM rapidly came to dominate (and which is still responsible for around a third of the ARM processors sold).

ARM has become the *de-facto* standard in the 32-bit embedded processor marketplace, powering the great majority of the consumer electronics products of the early 21st century.

6. A 20-year Perspective

A great deal of what happens in business, including high-tech business, cannot be put down to technology alone. The best technology often does not become the most successful product in the marketplace, and ARM's dominant position in the embedded processor market is the result of many factors, among which technological advantage plays at most a minor role.

So what are the lessons for computer science in general from the ARM story, if indeed there are any? In my view, the most fundamental is the one so often forgotten in the computing field: the high desirability of simplicity.

The RISC philosophy represented the return to basics in processor design that made the entire ARM project feasible.

Hermann Hauser, explaining the reasons for the success of the ARM, is quoted as asserting that the Acorn team had two advantages over the established industry at the time: (i) no money and (ii) no manpower. I am inclined to agree with this analysis. The very low resource available to the project made simplicity the highest imperative among the competing design criteria. I remember using the simplicity argument against all sorts of suggestions — if we let the design get at all complicated we would never finish it and it would never work if we did finish it. The final processor was indeed very simple, using fewer transistors than some 8-bit microprocessors and one-tenth the number used by some contemporary 16- and 32-bit processors.

Today's microprocessors (including some of the high-end ARM processors) have become ferociously complex. This is in part simply because the economics of chip design make it possible, and in part because we have so far failed to solve the problem of general-purpose parallelism, so it still makes some sense to add a lot of complexity to make a single thread go a bit faster. However, there is a dramatic paradigm shift underway in the microprocessor business with the end of the road for ever-faster uniprocessors having arrived, and already multicore processors dominate the new PC business. The software to exploit these multicore machines is lagging, but this is a problem that now must be solved!

Once we know how to program general-purpose multicore systems, where will it lead? My analysis is that what then matters is performance density (MIPS/mm^2 of silicon) and power-efficiency (MIPS/watt). On these measures simpler processors outperform their more complex brothers, so perhaps we will again see a return to simplicity in mainstream microprocessor design?

References

[1] D. A. Patterson and D. R. Ditzel, The case for the reduced instruction set computer, *Comput. Arch. News* **8**(6) (1980) 25–33.

[2] C. A. Mead and L. Conway, *Introduction to VLSI Systems* (Addison-Wesley, Reading, Massachusetts, 1979).

[3] S. B. Furber, *VLSI RISC Architecture and Organization* (Marcel Dekker, New York, 1989).

[4] S. B. Furber, *ARM System-on-Chip Architecture* (Addison-Wesley, Reading, MA, 2000).

Chapter 7

CARL ADAM PETRI AND "PETRI NETS"*

WILFRIED BRAUER

Institut für Informatik (17), Technische Universität München
Boltzmannstraße 3, D-85748 Garching bei München/Germany
brauer@informatik.tu-muenchen.de

WOLFGANG REISIG

Institut für Informatik, Humboldt-Universität zu Berlin
Unter den Linden 6, 10099 Berlin, Deutschland
reisig@informatik.hu-berlin.de

1. Introduction

Scientific tradition frequently names a fundamental notion, insight, or theory after its explorer or eminent representative. Typical examples include *"Abelian group"*, *"Planck's constant"* or *"Keynesian economic theory"*. Informatics occasionally names algorithms after their inventors, such as Dijkstra, Lamport or Floyd. Entire sub-fields of informatics are named after their respective persons only rarely. One of these few persons is *Carl Adam Petri*. Probably, every professional knows *"Petri Nets"* as a modeling technique. This paper will survey Petri's exceptional life and work.

Petri started his scientific career with his dissertation "Communication with Automata", which he submitted to the science faculty of Darmstadt Technical University in July, 1961. He defended his thesis there in June, 1962. [1]

In the rest of this paper, we first discuss this unusual and exceptional work, which laid the foundations for the success story of Petri Nets

---

*This paper has been adapted from an earlier paper published by the same authors in Informatik-Spektrum, Vol. 29, No. 5, pp. 369–374, Springer-Verlag, 2006.

including stimulations and challenges still to be taken up. We then consider the personal background of Carl Adam Petri and the pre-requisites and motivation for his work. We finish with the impact of Petri's dissertation and his other publications on the evolution of informatics.

Altogether, it will become transparent why some of Petri's ideas from the early 1960s had been taken up much later, and why some of his ideas are still pending for further elucidation and formalization.

2. The Dissertation

Since its publication in 1962, Petri's dissertation has been cited frequently (even though it probably has been read much less frequently).

This is not a conventional PhD dissertation, solving an open problem or elaborating a new theory. Instead, like in many later papers, Petri presented a wealth of ideas and proposals for revising the foundations of informatics. The text, thus, resembles sketches of a research program to some degree.

Nevertheless, as an excellent motivation for this fundamentally new approach, Petri starts out with an absolutely concrete and practical problem concerning the computation of recursive functions. The problem focuses on the observation, which was already well known in those years, that for a general recursive function f and an argument n, the amount of intermediate space necessary to compute $f(n)$ cannot be assessed in advance. Consequently, you cannot get hold of the required resources and then compute $f(n)$. Instead, you have to start out with a given set of resources. If the resources suffice, meaning that the computation of $f(n)$ terminates, it means that you have good luck. Otherwise, you have to assemble more resources and start again. Petri challenged the necessity of re-starting from scratch: can you not organize a computing system in such a way that fresh components can be allocated whenever necessary, and that the computation continues right away after adding components? Of course, the number of extensions must be unlimited and extensions should not significantly slow down the computation. Conventional computer architectures fail, as the following arguments show: each extension enlarges the system's overall size. This requires longer wires, in particular to the clock pulse. This, however, lengthens the runtime of the signals. Hence, the clock frequency must be reduced. Furthermore, the clock pulse generator's fan-out increases and consequently its power consumption increases without bounds. The clock frequency and power consumption of a switching element cannot be changed at will. Thus the clock pulse generator eventually collapses.

Therefore, the question arises whether there is an extendable architecture that does not need longer wires and which does not suffer from growing fan-out actually does exist. Petri has proven that this can be achieved by attaching each fresh component to that component having been attached previously. This construction comes with a price, since each component must be able to act autonomously and the entire system must work asynchronously.

As a feasibility study, Petri designed an asynchronous pushdown device composed of a sequence of modules, with each module containing a single data element and communicating with its two neighbors. The most recently attached module has one neighbor only. This way, a further fresh module can be attached. It is well known that two such devices suffice to implement a Turing Machine. Hence, Petri's construction is computationally universal! Petri presented this architecture at the first IFIP World Computer Conference in Munich, 1962. [2]

With the help of this thought experiment, Petri intended to show that asynchronous systems are more powerful than synchronous systems. From this insight, he deduced the consequence that a general theory of information processing, if intended to be practically relevant and not unnecessarily idealizing, *must* start out with asynchronous, locally limited operations. He concluded that it is therefore inappropriate to base the theory of informatics on sequential models.

In the course of his work, Petri employs a multitude of formal notations for asynchronous, distributed systems, including graphical representations and algebraic formulae with a "parallel" operator, in analogy to what later became process algebra. He additionally coined the basic notions of Petri Nets, i.e., "places" to describe local states and "transitions" for locally bounded actions.

Petri Nets — as they are known these days — first appeared in Petri's 1965 talk "Fundamentals on the description of discrete processes" at the 3rd Colloquium on Automata Theory in Hannover, 1966 [3]. However, at the end of 1964 already, the well-known software pioneer Tom DeMarco was exposed to Petri Nets at Bell Telephone Laboratories in the ESS-1 project (developing "the world's first commercial stored program telephone switch"). Tom was a member in the project's simulation team. In his contribution to the volume on "Software Pioneers" [4], DeMarco writes "Among the documents describing the simulation was a giant diagram that Ms. Hoover called a Petri Net (Ms. Erna Hoover ran the team). It was the first time I had ever seen such a diagram. It portrayed the system being simulated as a network of sub-component nodes with information flows connecting the nodes. In a rather elegant trick, some of the more complicated nodes were themselves portrayed as Petri Nets. ..." And some lines later: "The one document that we found ourselves using most was Erna's Petri Net. It showed how all the pieces of the puzzle were related and how they were obliged to interact. The lower-level network gave us a useful pigeon-holing scheme for information from the sub-system specs. When all the elemental requirements from the spec had been slotted by node, it was relatively easy to begin implementation. One of my colleagues, Jut Kodner, observed that the diagram was a better spec than the spec".

Petri did not just demand an adequate modeling technique for asynchronous distributed systems. His technique should additionally meet a number of further requirements.

First of all, Petri's modeling technique should obey the laws of physics. In particular, this implied giving up the fiction of global states. A discrete action of a system usually does not affect all system components, but only a few of them. An evident example is a computing step of an Internet-embedded computer: it is not adequate to conceive such a step as an update of the Internet's global state. Petri suggested that the *locality* of actions be modeled during system runs with utmost precision and to respect and exploit this aspect. Describing an action as a pair of an old state and a new state, as it is usually done, represents this aspect only implicitly. It is entirely inadequate to represent a single system run as a sequence of (global state occurrences and) action occurrences. Petri suggested that action occurrences not be ordered along a fictitious, idealized time scale, but by the partial order induced by the cause and effect relation instead. Two action occurrences a and b may remain unordered. This happens, when neither of them depends on the outcome of the other. Unorder then represents causal independence ("concurrency", in Petri's terminology). We observe that a may be causally independent of b, and b may be causally independent of c, with a causally before c. Hence, concurrency is not necessarily a transitive relation, in contrast to "temporally coincident". Relativity theory likewise assigns a "pre-cone" and a "post-cone" to each a. These cones consist of the action occurrences causally before and after a, respectively. Many years later this was re-detected and re-formulated in other system models by Lamport, Pratt, Gurevich, and others. The transfer of the idea of causal order from physics to informatics is a particularly impressive example of Petri's demand to design the theory of informatics in accordance with the laws of physics.

As a second requirement, Petri suggested to form models of informatics in the tradition of models of science. Profound scientific theory is rooted in *conservation laws.* Examples are the mass equations of chemistry or the energy conservation laws of physics. Elementary discrete actions should likewise obey a law of conservation. A typical necessary condition for conservation laws is the *reversibility* of processes. In informatics, this means for a step $S \xrightarrow{a} S'$ of an action a from a state S to a state S', that not only S' can be computed from S and a, but also S can be re-computed from S' and a as well. As an example, the assignment statement $x := x + 1$ is reversible, whereas $x := 1$ is not. Petri Net transitions are designed such that *local* causes and effects become evident and that they are reversible.

Petri's third requirement demands that a modeling technique should not only be adequate to describe implementable behavior, but it should also describe the human *pragmatic use* of computing systems. This aspect motivates the dissertation's ambiguous title "Communication with Automata": it covers humans communicating with automata, as well as the communication between different persons *with the help of* automata. Petri outlined these aims, together with ideas about how to attain them.

This was certainly not been a conventional dissertation – it was more to be conceived as a program of how to lay the foundations for the emerging science of informatics. This program however, was disconcerting in its long-term aims, and it contradicted prevailing ideas in its short-term proposals. So, it is easy to imagine that this piece of work caused its readers quite a headache. One of the leading pioneers of the first-generation electronic computers in Germany, Prof. Alwin Walter of Darmstadt Technical University, recognized the value of Petri's work and ensured that it was awarded as the best dissertation of his school in 1961/1962.

Petri's dissertation was also translated to English: in the context of the venture MAC at MIT, as part of Anatol W. Holt's "Information Systems Theory Project" [5].

3. Carl Adam Petri, The Man

Distributed and concurrent processes as the foundations of informatics, theoretical constructs in accordance with the laws of physical, conservation laws in analogy to science, formal modeling of the pragmatic use of computing systems — these were indeed exotic topics for the emerging science of informatics in the early 1960s, and rarely expected in a dissertation. Who is the person to dare build up his own scientific world, detached from current fashion and tendencies, but nevertheless respectful of the needs of practice and of scientific tradition?

Petri's biography was typical for his age-group in Germany, and it can be rapidly reported. Decisive experiences as a child and as a young man clearly influenced his scientific work later on.

Carl Adam Petri was born in Leipzig in 1926. He graduated in 1944 from the famous Thomas School and was immediately forced into military service. He was a British prisoner of war and remained in England until 1949. He then studied mathematics in Hannover and followed his teacher Heinz Unger as a PhD student to Bonn University. After receiving his PhD in 1962, he set up and ran the computer center of Bonn University, as well as the Institute for Information Systems Research at the "Gesellschaft fuer Mathematik und Datenverarbeitung" (GMD) in Birlinghoven (which later became an institute of Fraunhofer Society). He ran this institute until 1991. He turned down an offer for a position as a full-time professor at the University of Dortmund in 1973. During his entire career as well as after his retirement, Petri developed and published those ideas that he had already sketched out in his dissertation.

A number of reports and anecdotes help explain why Petri focused on very special scientific problems and methodological approaches. We will mention just three of them:

Petri's father had a PhD in mathematics and had met Minkowsi and Hilbert. He supported his son's interest in science. From a bankrupt bookseller's estate, Petri got two thick textbooks on chemistry on his 12th birthday, which he diligently worked through. His father arranged for his son to have an exceptional permit to use the Leipzig central library unrestrictedly. There he delved into publications of Einstein and Heisenberg.

Young Carl Adam as a flak auxiliary in the Air Force, observed officers who estimated the height, distance, and speed of approaching aircraft by simple means including visual judgment and hearing. The combination of measurement and estimation and mainly the quest for the responsibility for — inevitable — mistakes, has pre-occupied him and influenced much of his scientific work.

In his years in England, Petri solved some challenging land-measurement problems, such as the construction of concentric ellipses on rolling country.

The three topics mentioned, i.e., the methods of science, the pragmatic aspects of erroneous measurement, and the reasoning on geometrical objects, turn up again and again in Petri's later scientific work.

4. The Years Until 1980

Petri's dissertation was initially taken notice of, despite the important impact that we mentioned earlier on the representation of the ESS-1 system at Bell Labs, and its translation at MIT. This is hardly surprising, since the environment: computing technology at that time consisted of huge mainframe computers for numerical calculation, with punched paper tape and punch cards for input and output. A global clock seemed to be a natural course of action. Nobody thought about computer networks. Application software focused on numerical problems.

Since 1956 such software was mainly written in FORTRAN. The ALGOL 60 language initiated systematic research on the theory of *sequential* programs and sequential processes. Petri's proposal to organize input and output as parallel processes had been rejected. Missing I/O standards would hamper the success of ALGOL 60 later on. Applied informatics favored sequential processes. Mastering analog computers and asynchronous switching networks appeared to be difficult and too slow, despite their capability for parallel execution.

Theoretical informatics focused on sequential models for automata and computers, as well as on computable foundations, formal languages and compiler theory. In addition, highly speculative theoretical papers on "cybernetics" and "artificial intelligence" circulated, mostly without any realistic ideas on their realization (for example, speculations on a "general problem solver").

In contrast, Petri outlined the feasibility of his proposals by using the technology of that time. Even more, he discussed pragmatically the adequate use of this technology.

In summary, Petri's proposals came too early for applied informatics, and theory at that time focused on other topics. However, this poor response did not confuse or deter Petri. Together with his staff and numerous visitors, he strengthened his proposals in the sixties and seventies.

Still, in the sixties, he formulated several basic principles that have been re-invented by others later on. This includes alternating local states and steps (later in message-sequence-charts), side-effect free actions (later in functional languages) and multisets of tuples as states together with "put" and "take" replacing "write" and "read" (later in the "tuple space" of LINDA and in the Chemical Abstract Machine).

On the occasion of his acceptance speech for the Turing Award in 1991, Robin Milner stated that "Much of what I have been saying was already well understood in the sixties by Carl Adam Petri, who pioneered the scientific

modeling of discrete concurrent systems. Petri's work has a secure place at
the root of concurrency theory."

As a first breakthrough, MIT had considered Petri Nets in Project
MAC, at the end of the sixties. This successful project related to time-
sharing computer systems and "Multiple Access Computers" (and other
topics), reflected some of Petri's ideas. This gave rise to a line of research
that conceives Petri Nets as a mechanism to characterize classes of Petri
Nets with the help of formal languages. Some insight into Petri Nets can
be indeed gained in this way. But Petri was reluctant to appreciate such
results: he felt that they confuse concurrent and causally ordered event
occurrences, whereas Petri considers this distinction to be fundamental in
order to conceive systems properly. A number of theoretical results on Petri
Nets emerged in the seventies, in particular linear-algebraic methods to
compute system invariants.

Essentially, all theoretical results and applied case studies that were
available in the late seventies were compiled and presented at the First
Advanced Course on Petri Nets in Hamburg, 1979 (published as LNCS
84 [6]). In those years, distributed systems gained more attention and
alternative modeling and analysis techniques were suggested, including
process algebras and temporal logic.

5. The Years Since 1980

The number of publications on Petri Nets have grown sharply since the
early eighties. As an entirely new concept, the marking of places with sets of
uniform "black" tokens has been generalized to individual, "colored" tokens
of different kinds. This step increased the modeling power of Petri Nets
decisively, while structurally retaining the fundamental analysis technique,
in particular the linear algebraic calculi of place invariants and transition
invariants.

The eighties also saw a growing interest in distributed and reactive
systems, boosting not only Petri Nets, but a number of alternatives. Many
of them vanished without trace. The durable ones include the already
mentioned process algebras with Robin Milner's π-calculus of the 1990s,
as well as David Harel's Statecharts. Starting with Amir Pnueli's seminal
work in the late 1970s, temporal logic became the favorite analysis technique
of the field.

There is no clear evidence to what extent the graphical form of Petri
Nets may have influenced the graphical form of other calculi. The idea of

conceiving a distributed run as a partially ordered set of action occurrences has initiated *partial order model checking*: conventional model checking cannot cope with partially ordered runs, but only with total orders. A partial order, however, corresponds to a *set* of total orders. Some temporal logic properties hold for either all or none of those total orders in each set. So, it can effectively be tested for all total orders in a set by testing just one of them.

Petri Nets nowadays contribute to the actual discussion of model driven software design. Many currently favored modeling techniques include Petri Net-based components; most prominently the activity diagrams of UML2.

Meanwhile, Petri Nets are well established as a technique to model and to analyze embedded computer systems. A large community of scientists and software engineers employ Petri Nets in fairly different projects. Less known to computer scientists is the mechanical engineers' high esteem for Petri Nets. Carl Adam Petri has been awarded the 30th Werner-von-Siemens-Ring as a "scientist and designer of technology of outstanding merit". Petri is the second computer scientist who was honored with this prize (the first was Konrad Zuse). In his laudatory speech, Prof. Gottzein pointed out: "Petri Nets brought engineers a breakthrough in their treatment of discretely controlled systems. Petri Nets are a key to solve the design problem, as this is the first technique to allow for a unique description, as well as powerful analysis of discrete control systems. Based on Petri Nets, it is now possible to formulate system invariants for discrete systems".

Nowadays, a number of useful software tools are available, mutually linked with the help of the "Petri Net Kernel", to design and to analyze Petri Nets. Conferences are organized on a regular basis, in particular the annual "International Conference on Applications and Theory of Petri Nets", with satellite tutorials, workshops etc., since 1980. Meanwhile, the special interest group "Petri Nets and related system models" publishes a regular newsletter with almost 60 issues. The Computer Laboratory of the University of Hamburg organizes the Internet portal www.informatik.unihamburg.de/TGI/PetriNets/index.html with a wealth of current references to literature, tools, events etc.

6. Honors

With the establishment of Petri Nets as a recognized modeling technique in the eighties, Carl Adam Petri was honored many times. His outstanding awards include:

- 1988 — Verdienstkreuz 1. Klasse des Verdienstordens der Bundesrepublik Deutschland;
- 1988 — Honorary Professor at Hamburg University;
- 1989 — Member of Academia Europaea, London;
- 1993 — Konrad-Zuse-Medaille der Gesellschaft für Informatik, for distinguished credit for informatics;
- 1997 — Werner-von-Siemens-Ring, for outstanding merits for techniques in connection with science;
- 1997 — Member of the New York Academy of Sciences;
- 1999 — Honorary doctorate of the University of Zaragossa and
- 2003 — Commandeur in de Orde van de Nederlandse Leeuw.

7. What Will the Future Bring?

In his invited speech at the 26th International Conference on Application and Theory of Petri Nets, Miami, June 2005, Petri appreciated the diversity and the quality of the applications of his theory. But he called for a substantial expansion of the theory. Not for another "bunch" of Petri Net classes, or more sophisticated analysis algorithms, but for taking up the long-term aims as outlined in his dissertation. Much remains to be explored! It may be a matter of time until progress in hardware or demands of software will be strong enough to recall Petri's old proposals.

An example for such a long-term aim are the conservation theorems of information processing, in analogy to the preservation theorems of physics (such as Einstein's $e = mc^2$) or chemistry (such as equations like $NaJ + Cl \rightarrow NaCl + J$). Maybe — as Petri speculates — future software interfaces may be formulated in a much more abstract way, as well as more precisely, compared with today's state-of-the-art. This, however, would require that be developed a fundamental notion of what is preserved during dynamic information processing.

As a first approximation, Petri suggests a new concept of "information". Information *processing* then would mean to reshuffle the given information, while its *overall amount* remains constant. Apparently, none of the presently used notion of "information" would meet this requirement. It is yet entirely unknown whether or not there is a corresponding smallest unit of information. Up until now Petri is still looking for such concepts.

Informatics has evolved quite fiercely and in an unplanned manner, driven by its technological and economical potential. This kind of progression, together with today's common short-term projects, affects the structure of scientific development. Petri himself would not have stood a chance in this kind of environment. Only very few, such as he, ask long-term questions concerning the foundations of a systematic science of informatics.

References

[1] C. A. Petri, Kommunikation mit Automaten. Schriften des Rheinisch-Westfälischen Institutes für Instrumentelle Mathematik an der Universität Bonn Nr. 2, 1962.

[2] C. A. Petri, Fundamentals of a theory of asynchronous information flow, *Proceedings of the 1st IFIP World Computer Congress*, Munich, North Holland, 1962, pp. 386–390.

[3] C. A. Petri, Grundsätzliches zur Beschreibung diskreter Prozesse. 3. Kolloquium über Automatentheorie, Birkhäuser-Verlag, 1967, pp. 121–140.

[4] M. Broy and E. Denert (eds.), *Software Pioneers* (Springer-Verlag, Berlin, 2002).

[5] C. A. Petri, Communication with Automata. New York: Griffiss Air Force Base, Technical Report, RADC TR-65-377-Vol-1-Suppl-1 Applied Data Research, Princeton, NJ, Contract AF, 1966, 30(602) 3324.

[6] W. Brauer (ed.), Net theory and applications, *LNCS 84* (Springer-Verlag, Berlin, 1979).

Chapter 8

FROM STOCHASTIC MODELING TO OPERATIONAL ANALYSIS: THE JOURNEY BEGINS

JEFFREY P. BUZEN

Former Chief Scientist and Co-Founder, BGS Systems
National Academy of Engineering
Washington, D.C., USA
jeffbuzen@comcast.net

1. Stochastic Processes and the Central Server Model

I was introduced to queuing theory and stochastic modeling in the fall of 1969 during my third year of graduate study at Harvard. Having just returned after two years as a systems programmer at the National Institutes of Health in Bethesda, MD, I was eager to see if my experience in designing and building real-time systems for biomedical laboratories [1] could serve as the springboard for my PhD dissertation.

I experimented briefly with deterministic analysis of real-time scheduling, but soon found myself drawn to the mathematics of stochastic modeling. I quickly recognized that queuing models could provide a powerful tool for analyzing the type of performance issues I had encountered at NIH. In particular, I was interested in characterizing the factors that influence the overall throughput and response time of executing programs as they alternate between bursts of CPU processing and periods of delay while waiting for I/O transfers to complete.

In multi-programmed environments, several programs are typically executing at the same time, leading to the possibility of additional delays as programs queue for access to processors, I/O devices and main memory. Overloaded devices can become bottlenecks, queues can shift from one resource to another as devices are upgraded, and memory itself can become the bottleneck if there is not enough space to accommodate a sufficient number of active programs. I was interested in discovering the mathematical equations that govern these interactions, and it appeared to me that stochastic models provided the most promising avenue for pursuing this quest.

Other researchers had already demonstrated the value of queuing models for the analysis of algorithms that schedule processing requests for CPUs and I/O devices. However, these earlier models treated individual processing resources in isolation. There were no analytic models capable of representing the overall throughput and response time of typical programs (or transactions) flowing through a system and contending for CPUs and I/O devices while subject to constraints imposed by a limited amount of main memory.

The central server model, which formed the basis of my PhD dissertation [2], was the first analytic model capable of representing all these factors in an integrated fashion. I developed this model by thinking carefully about the life cycle of an idealized program, beginning with its arrival at a system and concluding when the program finally terminates. The set of processing resources that the program utilizes during its life cycle, its trajectory from resource to resource, and the points where queuing delays can occur because of contention with other programs, were all represented within the framework of this model.

Once I had formulated the central server model, the next step was to derive an analytic expression for the steady-state distribution of the underlying stochastic process. The steady-state distribution is important because, according to the Ergodic Theorem, this distribution can be used to predict the observable behavior of a real-world system operating over an interval of time (assuming that the real-world system is a realization of the underlying stochastic process, and that the interval of time is sufficiently long). This crucial connection between abstract mathematics and observable reality would later become one of my major concerns, but at the time I was happy to accept it without question and move ahead with the analysis.

Deriving the steady-state distribution involved solving a set of simultaneous linear equations. I was able to solve a small model with one CPU and two I/O devices by writing down the associated equations and applying basic algebraic techniques. While attempting to generalize my solution to larger models, I conducted a literature search and discovered that a general solution for the class of equations I was investigating had been published a few years earlier by Jackson [17] and by Gordon and Newell [16].

Although this was a great help, applying these results to the central server model left me with a "solution" expressed in terms of equations that were dauntingly complex and seemed computationally intractable. After studying these equations intensively for several months, I discovered a set of previously unknown recursive relationships within the closed form solution. These relationships enabled me to derive new closed form expressions for utilization, throughput, response time, and queue lengths. More significantly, these discoveries also enabled me to develop simple and highly efficient algorithms for computing the major quantities of interest. The new algorithms extended directly to a general class of queuing network models (not just the central server model), giving my work broader applicability than I had originally anticipated.

2. Early Concerns About Stochastic Modeling

Although I was quite satisfied with the theoretical content of my dissertation, I was also beginning to feel somewhat apprehensive about using steady-state stochastic processes as models of real-world phenomena. My concern was that stochastic processes were, in some ways, too powerful a tool for the task at hand.

For example, steady-state distributions are typically used to predict the average values one can expect to measure when observing systems for long intervals of time. They are also used to predict the observable distribution of time spent in each state. While these predictions seemed very reasonable to me, I was aware that steady-state stochastic processes could also be used to predict more exotic quantities such as the expected time between successive visits to a given state or the probability that the number of visits to a given state will exceed a certain threshold during some finite interval of time. At some point, I was concerned that the computation of these exotic quantities could become a mathematical exercise with little or no relevance to the values one could actually expect to encounter in the real world. Despite the established view that steady-state stochastic models were well suited for the analysis of real-world behavior, I was uneasy about pushing the mathematics too far.

I expressed these concerns on page 99 of my dissertation [2]: "The basic assumptions of the model regarding program behavior were assumed to be sufficiently realistic to permit the model to be of value in exploring the effect of queuing delays on system performance. However, this does not imply that these assumptions are sufficiently realistic to permit the model to be of value in further exploring program behavior itself. Hence, these derived results should not be interpreted as intrinsically useful information about program behavior in actual systems."

Even though I felt the central server model would be useful for predicting quantities related directly to the steady-state distribution such as throughput, response time, and queue length, I was trying to warn the reader that it would be dangerous to assume that the model was equally well suited for predicting detailed aspects of program behavior. At that time, I was unable to be more explicit about my warning. However, the problem of drawing a line between reasonable and unreasonable expectations regarding the accuracy of model predictions has evolved into one of my principal intellectual concerns for nearly four decades.

3. Impact of Empirical Success

The central server model quickly attracted the attention of experimentalists and practitioners in North America and Europe who were able to validate its predictive accuracy in a variety of real world settings [12, 13]. In an effort to better understand why the model worked as well as it did, I carried out a series of analyses [3, 4, 18] aimed at determining how sensitive the predictions were to the mathematical assumptions associated with the underlying stochastic process. I was still thinking that stochastic processes would be the best vehicle for modeling system performance. While studying one special case, I collaborated with the statistician Donald B. Rubin, my Harvard classmate and good friend, to derive a result that was essentially distribution-free [5]. Even then, our formulation of the model was still stochastic in nature.

My thinking began to change when I examined the way experimentalists were actually applying stochastic models. Generally speaking, almost all experimentalists operate using the same basic paradigm: they observe the behavior of a system during an interval of time, collect measurements during that interval, and then substitute the measured values into equations which are based upon the steady-state distribution of the model's underlying stochastic process. If the equations produce accurate results, the experimentalists conclude that the model is accurate.

At the time I was wrestling with these issues, Ugo Gagliardi and I were teaching a two semester graduate course on Operating Systems (Applied Math 251a & 251br) at Harvard. As part of the course, I presented several lectures each year on queuing theory and computer performance modeling.

During my first year of teaching this course (1971–1972), my lectures presented mathematical derivations of major results and then examined the implications of these equations for the performance of real-world systems.

Since class time was limited, I was trying to find a way to get through the derivations more quickly so I could spend more time on the applications. I knew that I could not simply ask my students to "trust me" when I asserted that the queuing equations were correct, but I also knew that understanding all the mathematical details required for a rigorous derivation was not necessarily going to help my students become better operating system designers. [It is interesting to note that Microsoft's co-founder Bill Gates audited AM 251a and then enrolled in AM 251br during his freshman year at Harvard (1973–1974). Perhaps, a detailed understanding of the way embedded Markov chains are used in the analysis of M/G/1 queuing models does contribute in some small way to success in the design of operating systems.]

4. Lectures at Serre Chevalier and Bologna

In any event, as I thought more deeply about the way experimentalists apply the results of stochastic models to the analysis of real-world systems, I began to realize that this might be the key to simplifying the way I presented these results to my students. Simplification became even more of a concern when I began presenting lectures on computer performance modeling at special "short courses" in various locations around the world. The first of these was organized by Professor Louis Bolliet of the University of Grenoble. It was held at Serre Chevalier in the French Alps in December 1974.

I wanted to present the same material that I covered in my course at Harvard, but I only had about half the time. To reach the main conclusions more efficiently, I decided to dispense with the usual stochastic modeling assumptions. Traditionally, I would begin my lectures on modeling by stating: Let us assume that system behavior can be represented by a steady-state stochastic process. At Serre Chevalier, I began with a simpler statement: Let us assume that we are observing the behavior of a real system operating over an interval of time. I was very happy with the way my lectures were received, and when I returned home I immediately began writing up my lecture notes so I could use them for another European meeting, which was scheduled for February 1975 in Bologna.

I completed my lecture notes in January. They were in fact published in a proceedings that was distributed at the Bologna meeting [6]. Here are some passages from these proceedings that illustrate the shift in my perspective:

A. The context for all the analytic derivations presented in the Bologna paper is defined in terms of an observer and an observation interval: *"Suppose that an observer records the behavior of such a system during a time period of length W."* (page 4)

B. I was interested in deriving relationships among values that an observer can, in principle, measure during the observation interval. These relationships were expressed as expected values since I was still working in a stochastic context. *"The expected amount of time the observer will find the system in state j is equal to $W \times P(j)$. Thus there is a direct and simple relationship between the steady state distribution and the empirical data an observer can expect to collect."* (page 4)

C. My derivations made use of the "flow conservation" assumption that is identical to the assumption we now call "flow balance": *"The number of times the token enters a particular node will thus equal the number of times it leaves that node during any period of length W. This observation is a specific example of a general principle known as the flow conservation law."* (page 6)

5. Emergence of Operational Analysis

Despite the very strong operational orientation of the Bologna paper, it was still written from a conventional stochastic perspective: the paper implicitly assumes that the ultimate objective of any rigorous queuing analysis is to derive equations that characterize the steady-state distribution of the underlying stochastic process. The operational arguments I presented in the Bologna paper are, in fact, the most critical steps in these stochastic derivations. However, I viewed these steps as being only part of the story. At the time the Bologna paper was written, I still believed it was necessary to add additional arguments to prove rigorously that the operational equations (pertaining to values that can be measured during a finite observation interval) can in fact be extended to the steady-state distributions of the underlying stochastic processes.

The fact that operational arguments are entirely sufficient to derive useful results within an alternative mathematical context (which I ultimately called Operational Analysis) did not occur to me until shortly after I returned from Italy. This realization represented a major turning point in my thinking. There was no longer any need to rely upon the assumption of an underlying stochastic process when deriving equations that characterize the observable performance of real systems as they operate over intervals of time. Operational solutions could be equally rigorous, while at the same time being directly applicable to problems of genuine interest to experimentalists and practitioners.

In March 1975, I began compiling a set of notes that formed the basis of the inaugural papers on Operational Analysis [7, 8]. Since I had already covered much of this material in my lectures at Serre Chevalier and Bologna, the mechanical process of writing down and deriving the "Fundamental Laws" was a straightforward algebraic exercise. However, articulating the essential nature of operational analysis and characterizing the principal differences between operational analysis and traditional stochastic modeling was, for me, a significantly more difficult challenge.

During the summer and fall of 1975, I had a number of vigorous discussions with colleagues regarding these issues. The most productive conversations were with Peter Denning and Erol Gelenbe (who had both attended the Bologna conference), and also with Don Rubin [7, 8].

The first formal publications on operational analysis, which appeared in the spring of 1976 [7, 8], presented relationships between average response time, average arrival rate, average queue length, average utilization, etc. Some earlier reviewers of these papers expressed the concern that operational analysis might be limited to relationships between interval-wide averages. I felt it was important to correct this view as soon as possible by demonstrating that operational analysis could also be used to derive expressions for complete distributions. Specifically, I focused on attained distributions that correspond to the fraction of time a system spends in each possible state.

To derive operational expressions for attained distributions, I simply re-visited the arguments presented in the Bologna paper, this time without any requirement to assume the existence of an underlying stochastic process. The Bologna paper followed the traditional stochastic approach of identifying the state transition diagrams ([6], page 5), assuming global balance is satisfied at each state as a consequence of the steady-state assumption ([6], page 6), and using the assumption of exponentially distributed service and inter-arrival times (memoryless processes) to conclude that certain conditional arrival and completion rates that appear in the state transition diagram must be state-independent ([6], page 8).

It was immediately clear to me that the structure of the state transition diagram corresponded directly to the observable behavior of a real system operating over an interval of time. In addition, the operational assumption of flow balance, which had already been introduced in the "Fundamental Laws" papers [7, 8], was sufficient to imply that the global balance equations must be satisfied. To complete the analysis of an M/M/1/N queue in an operational context, all I had to do was introduce new operational assumptions that would require the conditional arrival rates and service completion rates to be state independent.

These new operational assumptions, which I identified as "homogeneous arrivals" and "homogeneous service" [9], provided the basis for an operational derivation of the attained distribution of the M/M/1/N queue. This settled the concern that operational analysis might be limited solely to deriving relationships among interval-wide averages.

Over the next few months, I continued my efforts to clarify and articulate the essential nature of operational analysis and its relationship to stochastic modeling [10, 11]. I also collaborated with Peter Denning on a paper [14] that extended my earlier analysis of the M/M/1/N queue [9] to a general class of product form queuing networks. A year later, Peter and I collaborated on a tutorial paper [15] that assembled most of the previously published work on operational analysis into a single document, added a number of illustrative examples, and made the entire subject readily accessible to a large audience.

References

[1]   J. P. Buzen, Improving interrupt response time by software modification, *Proceedings of the IEEE Computer Group Conference*, Minneapolis, June 1969, pp. 143–147.

[2]   J. P. Buzen, Queuing network models of multiprogramming, Ph.D. dissertation, Harvard University, May 1971, 235 pages. (Republished in 1980 by Garland Press, NY in the series Outstanding Dissertations in the Computer Sciences.)

[3]   J. P. Buzen and A. W. Shum, Structural considerations for computer system models, *Proceedings of the Princeton Conference on Information Sciences and Systems*, Princeton, New Jersey, March 1974, pp. 335–339.

[4]   J. P. Buzen and P. S. Goldberg, Guidelines for the use of infinite source queuing models in the analysis of computer system performance, *Proceedings of the AFIPS National Computer Conference* **43**, May 1974, pp. 371–374.

[5]   J. P. Buzen and D. B. Rubin, Effects of compaction on memory utilization in multiprogramming systems, *Computer Architecture and Performance*, eds. E. Gelenbe and R. Mahl (North-Holland Publishing, Amsterdam, 1974), pp. 113–124.

[6] J. P. Buzen, Notes on queuing theory, *Proceedings of the International Seminar on Models and Measures for Computer Systems*, Gruppo Nazionale di Cibernetica e Biofisica of the Italian Research Council & IRIA — Institute de Recherche D'Inforrnatique et D'Automatique, Bologna, February 1975, pp. 1–38.

[7] J. P. Buzen, Fundamental laws of computer system performance, *Proceedings of the ACM Sigmetrics International Symposium on Computer Performance Modeling, Measurement and Evaluation*, Cambridge, Masachusetts, March 1976, pp. 200–210.

[8] J. P. Buzen, Fundamental operational laws of computer system performance, *Acta Inform.* **7**(2) (June 1976) 167–182.

[9] J. P. Buzen, Operational analysis: the key to the new generation of performance prediction tools, *Proceedings of the IEEE COMPCON 76*, Washington, DC, September 1976, pp. 166–171.

[10] J. P. Buzen, Modeling computer system performance, *CMG '76 Conference Proceedings*, November 1976, pp. 230–238.

[11] J. P. Buzen, Principles of computer performance modeling and prediction, *State of the Art Report on Performance Modeling and Prediction*, Infotech, Maidenhead, England, 1977, pp. 229–239.

[12] J. P. Buzen, From the central server model to BEST/1, *Performance Evaluation: Origins and Directions*, eds. G. Haring, C. Lindemann and M. Reiser (Springer, Berlin, 2000) pp. 485–489.

[13] J. P. Buzen, Milestones in the evolution of BEST/1, *Performance Evaluation — Stories and Perspectives*, ed. G. Kotsis (Austrian Computer Society, Vienna, 2003), pp. 11–26.

[14] P. J. Denning and J. P. Buzen, Operational analysis of queuing networks, in *Modeling and Performance Evaluation of Computer Systems*, eds. H. Beilner and E. Gelenbe (North-Holland, Amsterdam, October 1977), pp. 151–172.

[15] P. J. Denning and J. P. Buzen, The operational analysis of queuing network models, *ACM Comput. Surv.* **10**(3) (September 1978) 225–261.

[16] W. J. Gordon and G. F. Newell, Closed queuing systems with exponential servers, *Oper. Res.* **12**(2) (April 1967) 266–277.

[17] J. R. Jackson, Jobshop-like queueing systems, *Manage. Sci.* **10**(1) (October 1963) 131–142.

[18] A. W. Shum and J. P. Buzen, The EPF technique: A method for obtaining approximate solutions to closed queuing networks with general service times, *Modeling and Performance Evaluation of Computer Systems*, eds. H. Beilner and E. Gelenbe (North-Holland, Amsterdam, October 1977), pp. 201–220.

Chapter 9

FROM ROCKET CONTROL TO VIRTUAL DESIGN

OLIVIER PIRONNEAU

Université Pierre et Marie Curie
Laboratoire Jacques-Louis Lions
Olivier.Pironneau@pmc.fr

Applied mathematicians, such as John Von Neumann, have had a great influence on the design of computers and have adapted them to their need such as optimal control of trajectories, game theory and the numerical study of fluid flows. Ordinary differential equations and optimization problems were among the first to be solved after the Fortran language came into being, but computational fluid dynamics took much longer to mature, and still one cannot say that the partial differential equations of fluid mechanics are solvable using today's computers. For this reason such open problems continue to influence computer architectures. Nevertheless it is now possible to design a virtual aircraft prototype entirely and fairly accurately, and the impact of this technology is felt even more on software development for Computer Aided Design systems. This paper is a short history of the interaction between numerical simulations in engineering, and the development of hardware and software over the past thirty years based on the author's personal experience.

1. Computational Fluid Dynamics

From the very early age of computing up to the end of the cold war, Computational Fluid Dynamics was given top priority because of its applications to the design of fighter aircraft, and to the simulation of nuclear explosions.

The fundamental equations of fluid dynamics, the Navier Stokes equations, are non linear partial differential equations (partial differential equations). They admit a number of simplifications corresponding to potential flow, boundary layer flow, Euler flow, etc. For airplanes each is useful in its own regime but ultimately the full compressible Navier-Stokes

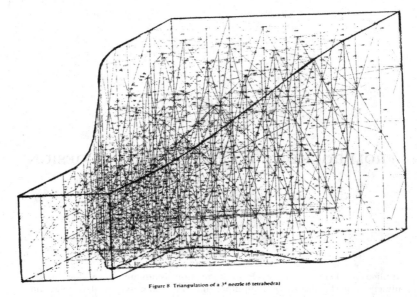

Fig. 1.1. The "tetrahedrisation" of a nozzle for the computation of a potential 3D flow in 1973 on an IBM 360 (courtesy of J. Periaux [11]).

equations with turbulence modeling are necessary, together with sensitivity analysis, in order to carry out design improvements and optimizations for advanced aircraft (see Fig. 2.1).

By 1970 computers could solve fairly accurately large classes of optimization problems and ordinary differential equations. I had myself solved two of these in 1969 on a small computer which seemed to be used by no one else in the Electrical Engineering and Computer Science Department at the University of California, Berkeley. Thus I was almost using a personal computer! The program was typed on a paper ribbon or input directly on the console and, of course, a single spelling mistake was heavily punished.

The partial differential equations of solid mechanics were among the first to be solved numerically using the Finite Element Method and in three dimensions even in the sixties; but translating the technique to fluid flows had not yet been done. Thus in those early days scientists at NASA, ONERA, the Los Alamos Laboratory and others where using the finite difference method [7] which is an extension of the tools developed for the ordinary differential equations of rocket trajectory calculations.

The finite difference method is not adapted to the complex shape of airplanes.

At Dassault Aviation in France, P. Perrier was a strong promoter of numerical simulation because he saw it to be the only way to compete with the American industries which had much larger resources for wind tunnel testing. However the constraint was to use an arbitrary mesh. Among the first to solve a flow around an entire wing in 3D was J. Periaux at Dassault on an IBM 360; an example is shown on Fig. 1.1).

The Fortran IV language was used at that time via punched cards; graphics were displayed with a pen plotter, mostly on Benson tables, and we note that Benson was a French company.

At IRIA at the same time, during the period running from 1974 to 1988, the institute's mainframe computer was not connected to the Benson plotting table and a tedious manual data transfer on tape had to be used resulting in endless delay and which required much good will on the part of the computer operators. Personal computers, the Apple II in 1978 in my case, were paving the way to a final relief from the arrogant abuse that some of us had to experience on the part of some computer centers.

The situation improved considerably at the end of the seventies with the advent of remote graphic terminals connected to virtual memory time-sharing systems, the Honeywell-Bull Multix machine, which in my case meant the possibility of using a local Tektronics graphic display which was remotely connected to the time-sharing computer system. At this time computations for an entire aircraft covering compressible potential flow — a world premiere — were conducted at Dassault-Aviation with our collaboration (see Fig. 1.2). This was followed soon after by A. Jameson's finite volume solution of Euler's equation around an almost complete aircraft frame [5].

Later the Apollo workstation made the biggest and final revolution in the laboratory; now the CPU and the graphics were tightly integrated in one machine and consequently greatly increased the number of computer runs that one could accomplish per day. Most importantly, people such as I became the operators of the computing resource and we were then motivated to learn much more about Computer Science itself, rather than just being numerical users of a remote computing resource.

This type of powerful workstation was used in competition, or in addition to, the minicomputers that were already commonly available at that time. Every decent Computational Fluid Dynamics laboratory had to acquire one of these expensive machines: a budget constraint that forced us to hunt for industrial contracts, in itself not a bad thing after all, but also a significant strain on the frontier between applied research and commercial

Fig. 1.2.   Compressible potential flow over an entire aircraft computed in 1980 [3] on an ibm 370 by the Finite Element Method, courtesy of Dassault Aviation.

services. At that time, the technical stress was on mesh generation and three-dimensional graphic tools, as much as on algorithmic speedup.

Since then, the working environment has not changed much. We still use powerful computer graphics on desktop machines with the possibility to defer computing to parallel clusters or mainframes supercomputers. However these set-ups are no longer a financial burden to most laboratories, and CFD is available to everyone at the cost of a top end personal computer.

2. Open Problems

After fifty years of numerical research, turbulence is still not fully understood. Depending on the situation one may choose to use Reynolds averaged Navier-Stokes equations or large eddy simulations [12] or Direct eddy simulations models with no certainty about the level of precision that may be attained for a given problem. Better results are often synonymous with bigger meshes, and there is still a great need for faster computers and more sophisticated algorithms.

It is now also possible to treat coupled problems, or so called "multiphysics". For instance, it is possible to study the interactions between air flows and the structure of an aircraft when it turns, or of the aircraft's electromagnetic reflections during flight for radar studies, as illustrated in Fig. 2.2. Perhaps one day in the near future we may see a numerically

Fig. 2.1. Pressure color map from a RANS calculation [6] on a business jet performed in 1998 on a workstation (computed by Bijan Mohammadi).

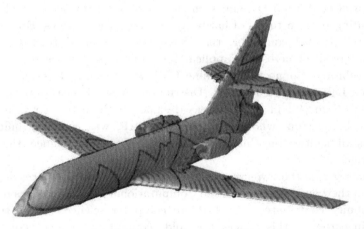

Fig. 2.2. Electromagnetic impact on a business jet computed on a parallel cluster by an integral formulation and the fast multipole method with Domain Decomposition in 2004 on a PC cluster 32 CPU (computed by Pascal Have).

perfectly optimized aircraft using active devices on deformable wings to provide less drag. This short history has shown the importance of meshes and graphics, and jokingly some have said that Computational Fluid Dynamics has the same initials as "color fluid dynamics". The present importance of Computer Aided Design systems could also have been predicted. Currently fluid flow modules and advanced mesh generation are not well embedded in Computer Aided Design systems, but we expect they will soon be. Also Computer Aided Design system developers are pressed to include parallelism and task decompositions because of multiple core processors are becoming common in high performance computing engines and, more surprisingly, because of the cooperative effort that is required in the design of an aircraft; the problems encountered by aerospace companies such as EADS with its dual head leadership and its difficulties with subcontractors illustrate the importance of modular and concurrent engineering.

Despite all of these unsolved problems, forty years of research have made possible the design of an aircraft without extensive wind tunnel testing, and the author himself would be quite willing to fly in such an "untested" vehicle: it is safe!

3. Computational Fluid Dynamics and Computer Science

Computational Fluid Dynamics has had a strong influence on high speed computing both in terms of hardware and on software tools. For instance the first parallel computer, the University of Illinois' ILLIAC IV [8], was designed for aerospace applications. One important customer of the the celebrated Connection Machine CM5 was the US Government's Los Alamos Laboratory. The DAP (Distributed Array Processors) at Queen Mary College [10] in the UK was designed with meteorology in mind; Bjarne Stroustrup, who worked on the DAP, was certainly influenced by his difficulties on this machine when he later designed the C++ language.

However, in the seventies and the eighties, teams of computer designers lived in their own world, while the Computational Fluid Dynamics research community contributed very little to computer science. As we tried to explain earlier in this article, the "old" computing centers were "just a window and a counter" for the end user to submit punched card stacks.

Having have worked on a variety of computers, and suffered greatly from their limitations, this author first learned computer assembly language at the University of California at Berkeley in 1969, the only time one could access the punch card room without queuing was at 3 am! At D.A.M.T.P. in Cambridge, UK, in 1971 no one was interested in computing so we had the access terminal for ourselves and the working conditions were good but it was impossible to make a decent graphical plot directly from computer output. At IRIA in 1974, still then a rich institute with a large Honeywell mainframe computer, it was impossible to access any documentation and the driver software for the Benson plotting table was never written. That no one assigned this as a summer project for a computer science class illustrates well enough the ivory tower in which fundamental system design people were living in.

In 1978 being the head of the computer center at the university of Paris 13, I was determined to stop such abuse, and it was not a small task. For instance, one day an operator threw the card deck of a student on the floor because it wasn't tidy enough to his taste. Basically the situation changed when personal computers arrived, to the great fear of the operators who immediately sensed the danger and refused to install them in our computer center.

At Dassault-Aviation, the computing center was a true service but there too no one was allowed to tamper with the system, if ever one was tempted to struggle with the Job Control Language!.

The plunge of sophisticated users into computer science only came with the minicomputer era in the eighties. Partial Differential Equation solution software packages began to appear, such as Nastran for solid mechanics [9]. For fluid mechanics, Phoenix and Fidap were fairly successful Fortran language based packages, but they would produce output for specific graphics like the Tektronics terminal. The fight of the day was to be able to port the code on a variety of hardware without having graphic standards such as OpenGL, and without a user interface. This is to be compared with today's advanced finite element software such as Abaqus[1] which can be interfaced with Computer Aided Design tools such as Catia [4] and customized with Python scripts.

Many researchers trained in Computational Fluid Mechanics went into computer graphics, and the first Computer Aided Design Systems was born in the French Laboratory LIMSI at Université Paris-Sud; so finally users were contributing to the user-friendliness of their machines through:

- Unified geometry input languages,
- Automatic mesh generators (EMC2 for example),
- Versatile libraries of flow solvers, and
- Visualization packages.

One important item was still missing: a unified job submission system. This came with the Unix, DOS and Mac OS operating systems. Strangely enough at that time only a few Computational Fluid Dynamics scientists saw the potential of personal computers, and yet 20 years later this is their most preferred tool. Since then, the contribution of this community to computer science is much more visible: numerical analysts push the limits of languages such as C++ and invent new concepts such as "straights", "generic programming", and optimized templated libraries such as Blitz [2]. Furthermore most of the algorithms for the parallelization of a single task have been developed in the context of partial differential equation simulations (such as OpenMP, PVM, and MPI).

This fruitful interaction between super computing and the design of computers is not likely to stop. At present in centers for research in nuclear physics, which are often equipped with the largest available computers, software which is potentially useful to many communities of users is being developed, offering capabilities such as high speed retrieval of large data sets, break points in parallel programs for effective recovery and restart, parallel visualization, and multithreading/domain-decomposition optimizers.Thus numerical science is finally contributing significantly to the areas of high performance computing and computer science, areas on which numerical science depends critically for its ability to move forward in answering key problems in science and engineering.

References

[1]   Abaqus Inc: Abaqus products overview (www.abaqus.com)

[2]   Blitz: The Scientific C++ libray blitz, (www.oonumerics.org/blitz)

[3]   M. O. Bristeau, R. Glowinski, J. Periaux, O. Pironneau and P. Perrier, On the numerical solution of nonlinear problems of fluid mech. by least squares, *Comp. Meth. in Appl. Mech* **17/18** (March 1979).

[4]   Catia: www.3ds.com/products-solutions/plm-solutions/catia/ overview

[5]   A. DAP, J. Baker and N. Weatherhill, Calculation of the inviscid transonic flow over a complete aircraft, *AIAA* paper 86-0103 (1986).

[6]   B. Mohammadi and O. Pironneau, *The K-epsilon Turbulence Model* (J. Wiley, 1994).

[7]   D. Ritchmeyer and K. W. Morton, *Difference Methods for Initial Value Problems* (Interscience, New York, 1967).

[8]   G. H. Barnes, R. M. Brown, M. Kato, D. J. Kuckand, D. L. Slotnick and R. A. Stokes, The ILLIAC IV computer, *IEEE Trans. Comput.* **17**, 746–757 (1968).

[9]   T. G. Butler and D. Michel, NASTRAN: A Summary of the functions and capabilities of the NASA structural analysis computer system, Scientific and Technical Information Office, NASA (1971).

[10] D. Parkinson, The Distributed Array Processor (DAP), *Computer Physics Communications*, **28**, (1983) 325–336.

[11] J. Periaux, Three dimensional analysis of compressible potential flows with the finite element method, *Int. J. Numer. Methods. in Eng.* **9**, (1975) 775–831.

[12] P. Sagaut and C. Meneveau, *Large Eddy Simulation for Incompressible Flows: An Introduction*, Scientific Computation series (Springer, 2005).